# PLANNING A BETTER
# KITCHEN

**CREATIVE HOMEOWNER PRESS®**

# CONTENTS

Based on *Creating a Home,*
First Edition © Eaglemoss Publications Limited 1986, 1987, 1988

Printed at Webcrafters, Inc.
Madison, Wisconsin, U.S.A.

Current printing (last digit)
10 9 8 7 6 5 4 3 2 1

Creative director: Warren Ramezzana
Editor: Kimberly Kerrigone
Copy Editor: Carolyn Anderson-Feighner
Cover Photograph: Smallbone of Devizes
Kitchen Design Consultant: David Ulrich, CKD; Ulrich Inc.
Library of Congress Catalog Number: 91-071689
ISBN 0-932944-97-3 (paper)

CREATIVE HOMEOWNER PRESS® BOOK SERIES
A DIVISION OF FEDERAL MARKETING CORP.
24 PARK WAY
UPPER SADDLE RIVER, NJ 07458-2311

# INTRODUCTION

Creating a kitchen that looks good and works well takes more than money. You need a basic knowledge of kitchen planning, information about what equipment is on the market, and ideas.

**Planning a Better Kitchen** gives you all of these. It is packed with color photographs of kitchens of every style, shape and size, backed up by drawings and scale plans showing how they can be rearranged to suit different needs. And a fully illustrated, up-to-date guide on choosing new equipment covers everything from built-in units and ranges to sinks and faucets.

There is no one 'ideal' kitchen. What is perfect for you depends on your personal lifestyle. To help you establish your personal priorities, a comprehensive questionnaire is included. The first and vital stage of any project is planning the layout. This is the key to making your kitchen workable. After mapping out the ground rules for positioning kitchen units and appliances, there are five separate chapters on the typical kitchen layouts: the L-shape, the U-shape and the one-wall, the big kitchen with an island layout and the small kitchen in which not an inch of space is wasted.

No detail of kitchen planning is overlooked. Further chapters cover the all-important matters of storage; planning pleasant and efficient lighting; using color to create the atmosphere you want; what materials to choose for countertops and backsplashes; even how to make use of spaces between units.

Whether you are planning to completely remodel or just wondering what sort of new range to buy, the fully illustrated review of kitchen units and appliances presents all the options to help you make the right decision. It covers all the latest equipment on the market: ranges of every kind, microwaves, refrigerators and freezers, built-in kitchen units and accessories, sinks and faucets, waste disposers, range hoods, exhaust fans and dishwashers.

Finally, there are chapters on planning and furnishing a laundry room, including an illustrated guide to washers and dryers.

**Planning a Better Kitchen** is an essential guide to remodeling or replanning your kitchen to suit today's needs.

# CLASSIC KITCHEN LAYOUTS

## A kitchen, above all else, is a place of work. Plan to make that work easy and efficient and it will be enjoyable too.

Surprising as it may seem, the efficient use of a kitchen depends more on how it is laid out than how big it is. Although many people long for something larger, small kitchens have plenty of potential, given the right layout.

**The work sequence** When you are planning the kitchen you should always aim to make the food storage, the preparation, the cooking and the serving areas as practical and energy-saving as possible.

A great deal of research has been carried out into the most efficient way to arrange a kitchen. Cooking a meal follows a predictable pattern. The three main areas of activity are food storage – refrigerator and food cupboards; preparation – countertops and sink; and range and cooktop.

Although you often have to double back on yourself, expert planners have established that the most sensible layout should follow this pattern: refrigerator/countertop/sink/countertop/range and cooktop/countertop. If it is possible this should be arranged from left to right in an unbroken sequence.

### THE WORK TRIANGLE

The sequence of storage, preparation and cooking is known as the work triangle. Obviously, the dimensions of the triangle vary, depending on the size and shape of the kitchen but the basic concept should be applied to the design of every kitchen.

Ideally, the total length of the three sides of the triangle should be between 13 and 23ft. Distances any greater will only create extra kitchen mileage; any less will leave you feeling cramped.

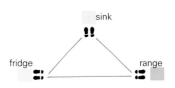

**The classic layouts** A kitchen can be almost any shape or size, depending on the architecture of the building. But there are just six basic layouts that, working within the guidelines of the work triangle, will give you a practical kitchen that is a pleasure to work in.

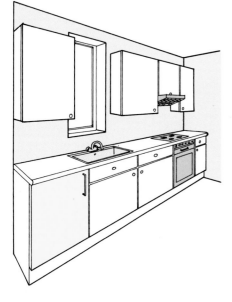

◁ *The one-wall*
*Suitable for one or two people, this kitchen can be built into a very narrow space. The units and appliances are all lined up along one wall. Place the sink in the middle and*

*choose built-in appliances so you don't lose any of the limited counter space. The room should be at least 6½ft. wide to allow enough space for two people to pass each other. The one-wall kitchen is often a corridor and through traffic can be a problem.*

*Eating will have to take place elsewhere, unless a pull-out or fold-down unit can be incorporated.*

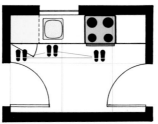

scale: 1 square = 1 sqaure yard

▷ *The double galley*
*Similar to the one-wall, the double galley has units lined along facing walls.*

*Most layouts will be dictated by the position of existing doors and windows but, ideally, the sink and range/cooktop should be on one side, with the refrigerator and storage opposite.*

*The double galley is a compact and easy layout for one or two people to work in, but make sure there is at least 4ft. between facing units, otherwise bending down to get something from*

*a low-level cupboard becomes difficult. Traffic can be a problem if there are doors at both end of the room.*

scale: 1 square = 1 square yard

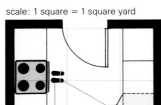

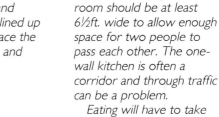

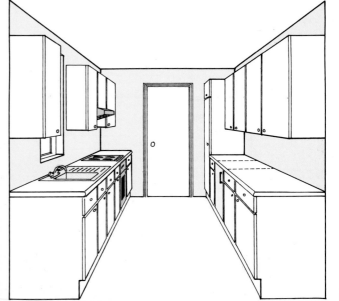

## ▷ The L-shape

This is a very versatile layout. The units and appliances are arranged on two adjacent walls, creating an efficient work triangle protected from through traffic.

Make sure that the corner is used to its fullest potential – a built-in carousel in the corner cupboard is a good solution. Separate the sink, range/cooktop and refrigerator with stretches of countertop to avoid the areas of activity becoming too congested.

The sides of the L can be adapted to suit an awkwardly shaped room and should be able to accommodate two cooks fairly comfortably.

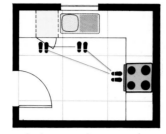

scale: 1 square = 1 square yard

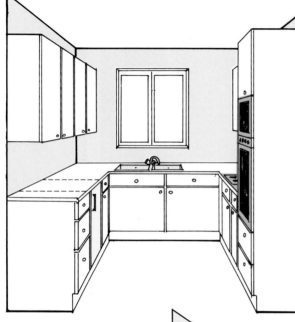

## ◁ The U-shape

The best kitchen layout of all, the U-shape has three walls for units and appliances, uninterrupted by through traffic – an efficient and safe arrangement in a compact area.

Scale is important: you need enough space between facing units to allow two people to work without banging into each other, while too large a space leads to unnecessary walking around. The flexible shape can often accommodate a dining area with ease.

scale: 1 square = 1 square yard

## ▷ The peninsula

In a larger room, or kitchen/dining room, the peninsula is a flexible layout. The short arm jutting out into the room divides the cooking and eating areas; it can be used to house a sink or cooktop with an efficient exhaust hood above, or it can be a breakfast bar or serving area.

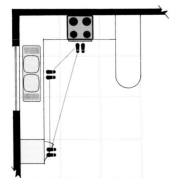

## ▽ The island

Essentially, the island layout is a larger version of the L- or U-shape with an additional work area in the middle. It can look stunning but is only practical in a spacious room. Careful planning is required.

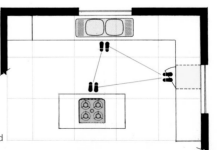

scale: 1 square = 1 square yard          scale: 1 square = 1 square yard

# KITCHEN CHECKPOINTS

## Spend time carefully assessing your needs when designing a new kitchen.

Installing a new kitchen is a major outlay and a long-term investment. Don't approach the venture in too much of a hurry as any mistakes at the planning stage will prove costly as well as a nuisance to the user.

The plan below gives you an at-a-glance guide to the main considerations in good kitchen design and the next page is a questionnaire to help organize your thoughts in detail before you start.

Keep work triangle down to a minimum, usually not more than 23ft. and no shorter than 13ft.

Task lighting provided by strip lights under wall units – there must also be adequate background lighting.

Double bowl sink – one bowl taking garbage disposer. This allows for washing up and still leaves room for vegetable preparation and use of faucets.

Wall and base end shelves for storage jars and cook books.

Food storage – refrigerator, etc. – near to preparation area.

24in. countertop to accommodate refrigerators, dishwashers, etc.

Tall storage for brooms and cleaning materials should not interrupt work surface runs – keep tall units together.

Deep drawers under cooktop for pan storage.

To minimize complications with plumbing, the sink, washing machine and dishwasher are near to water supply.

Adequate electrical outlets – at last one double outlet for each working area.

Oven opening area a minimum width of 16in.

Range hood vented outside or can be recirculating if not on outside wall.

Swing out racks inside corner cupboard for easy access.

# KITCHEN CHECKLIST

A kitchen that works and looks just the way you want it to is not easy to achieve. It requires a detailed analysis of your needs, a careful assessment of the potential of the space and a thorough investigation of the merchandise available to implement your ideas. You must also always bear in mind the basic principles of kitchen planning.

Designing a kitchen is a complicated and intricate procedure, which with our guidance you should be able to do for yourself. Professional help is now available from many retail outlets free of charge but no professional kitchen planner can help you unless you first work a bit at helping yourself. This is essential as the professional design solutions provided by planners can only be as good as your briefing.

The questionnaire below is designed to help you clarify your thoughts and to get your ideas into a workable form.

## FAMILY/LIFESTYLE

- ☐ What do you and your family like about your present kitchen?
- ☐ What don't you like about the kitchen you have now?
- ☐ What is your idea of a dream kitchen?
- ☐ Who uses the kitchen and how old are they?
- ☐ How many people tend to use the kitchen at the same time?
    You'll need more space if two or three people often combine to help with cooking and cleaning up, or if toddlers or young children are to play in the kitchen.
- ☐ Does anyone using the kitchen have special needs? For example, is the cook left-handed?
- ☐ Is anyone in the family elderly or disabled?
- ☐ Do you have pets that eat or sleep in the kitchen regularly?

## EATING

How often and what kind of meals are taken in the kitchen and for how many people?
- ☐ Breakfast only.
- ☐ Snacks.
- ☐ All meals.

What kind of eating facilities are needed/preferred?
- ☐ A table for sit-down meals.
- ☐ A fold-down table.
- ☐ A bar with stools.
- ☐ A serving pass-through to the dining room.

## ACTIVITIES IN THE KITCHEN

What takes place in the kitchen, apart from storing, preparing and cooking food and cleaning up?
- ☐ Eating.
- ☐ Laundry.
- ☐ Leisure activities such as watching TV, listening to music, reading, or hobbies that might involve using the sink or range.
- ☐ Homework.
- ☐ Entertaining.

## BUDGET

- ☐ How much money is available to spend on your new/improved kitchen?
- ☐ How is finance to be provided?
    A new kitchen is a major home improvement/investment. It should last for many years. It may be worthwhile raising extra finance (for example, by extending your mortgage or applying for a loan) to give yourself the kitchen you really want.
- ☐ Are you thinking of moving within the next few years?
    If so, avoid the temptation to overspend. A new kitchen adds a certain amount of value to a house, but usually not as much as the kitchen itself costs. The next occupants may well have very different ideas of what a kitchen should be like.

## STYLE

- ☐ What style are you aiming to create?
- ☐ What color schemes appeal to you?
    Choice of colors will be influenced by the type of light your room receives as well as personal preference. Kitchens with a cold tone tend to feel friendlier when decorated in warm colors; while those with a warmer tone can take cooler ones. Some people find cooler colors more calming and relaxing to work with; others respond more positively to the lively nature of warm colors like red.
- ☐ What type of flooring do you prefer?
- ☐ What wallcovering?

## SPACE/STRUCTURE

- ☐ Can you work within the space available?
- ☐ Can you find ways of providing more space?
- ☐ Can you take in space from an adjacent area such as a walk-in pantry, a large hall or a little-used dining room?
- ☐ Would removal of the wall between kitchen and living area provide an open plan arrangement to give more space for kitchen activites?
- ☐ Can you expand your kitchen area with an extension to your house?
- ☐ Could you resite your kitchen in a larger room?
    Always obtain professional advice before carrying out any structural alterations.
- ☐ How much work surface will you need, and what type do you like?
    Consider the work surface height. This is usually dictated by the dimensions of appliances but if you are very tall or small you can adjust the height by using plinths.

## APPLIANCES

- ☐ What kind of fuel do you plan to use?
- ☐ Gas.
- ☐ Electric.
- ☐ Solid fuel.
- ☐ A combination.
- ☐ What type of cooking appliances will you have?
- ☐ How many small electrical appliances will you have, or plan to have in the future? You will need sufficient electrical outlets and storage space.
- ☐ What combination of refrigerator and freezer will you have?
- ☐ Do you use a lot of frozen food?
    If you do, obviously you need a large freezer. Perhaps it would be better kept out of a kitchen, in a basement or garage.

## SINKS

- ☐ What arrangement of sink(s) is best suited to your needs/space/budget?
- ☐ A single sink.
- ☐ A double sink.
- ☐ An extra half sink.
- ☐ Where do you want the draining boards?
    Consider whether you prefer to clean up from left to right or right to left; or if you want drainers on both sides.
- ☐ Do you not have room for a very large garbage bin in the kitchen?
    Consider installing a garbage disposer.
- ☐ Where could you site a draining rack? If possible, attach this to the wall to save counter space.
- ☐ Do you want a dishwasher, now or in the future?
    Make sure you plan adequate space and plumbing to save additional work later.
- ☐ Is there enough storage space near the sink for cleaning materials, mops and buckets, towels, etc?

## STORAGE

- ☐ How much food/equipment must your kitchen contain?
    Think about all the kinds of food you have to keep in the kitchen. This will guide you toward the size of refrigerator/freezer needed and amount and size of cupboards/ shelves required. Think about a pantry.
- ☐ How about utensils and pots and pans?
- ☐ Where are you going to keep your crockery, cutlery, glasses?
    All these considerations will determine what sort of cupboards you need. Look through manufacturers' catalogs and visit a few showrooms to see the vast choice available. Consider carousel cupboards and deep, wire drawers as well as traditional shelves and cupboards.

## LIGHTING AND VENTILATION

What kind of lighting do you prefer?
- ☐ General overhead light.
- ☐ Fluorescent strips behind diffusers.
- ☐ Clusters or strips of spotlights.
- ☐ Electrified tracks.
- ☐ Recessed downlights.
- ☐ Special under-cupboard lighting.

Is there adequate ventilation in the kitchen?
- ☐ Should you consider a range hood or an exhaust fan over the range or cooktop?

## LAUNDRY

- ☐ What kind of washing machine will there be?
- ☐ Will there be a dryer? Will it be stacked or adjacent to the machine, or a combined system to save space?
- ☐ Is there enough space for detergent, laundry basket, drying rack?
- ☐ What facilities will you need for ironing? Where will you keep the ironing board and iron?
- ☐ Could the laundry be sited in the bathroom or a separate utility room?

# PLANNING A BUILT-IN KITCHEN

## An accurate plan with everything worked out will save tears when it comes to organizing a kitchen.

Before you decide on what appliances and units to have in your kitchen, and what style you like, you need to work out exactly how everything is going to fit in the right place.

The first stage is to get an accurate, scaled floor plan of the room on graph paper.

Measuring for a built-in kitchen calls for more accuracy than any other room. Watch out for uneven flooring and corners that appear to be square but in fact are not 90°; care will have to be taken, especially when sizing corner cupboards or appliances.

Make a list of all the appliances you plan to have and their dimensions, making allowances for pipes, wires and ventilation at the back. Make scaled cut-outs for each appliance, and move them around on your plan, following the work triangle principles set out on pages 7-8, until you find the best possible layout for your kitchen.

Make cutouts of the units too, and add them to your plan. There are different sizes available; the choice varies according to the manufacturer but, usually, the more expensive the range, the more choice you will have.

Once you have finalized your plan, it's a good idea to stick masking tape down on the floor where all the cupboards and appliances are to go to check that the layout works.

If new plumbing, drainage or wiring is involved, check that your plans conform to regulations.

## CUPBOARD UNITS

Wall and floor units usually come in standard widths starting at 8in. and increasing in 4in. steps to 24in. for single cupboards and 48in. for double units.

Wall cupboards are almost always 12in. deep and floor units are either 20in. or 24in. deep. Most appliances are 24in. deep; so choose the same size cupboard if you plan to build in the appliances. Alternatively, you could set all the floor units slightly in from the wall, using a deeper work surface to cover the gap at the back, this is ideal if you are likely to end up with plumbing that would be best concealed behind the units.

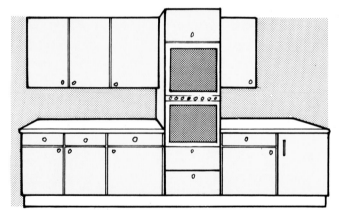

*▷ Corners* are the trickiest areas to deal with. It is very important that doors don't open into each other.

If you are housing an appliance near a corner, you must be able to open the door to its fullest extent without banging into the wall. Here, extra tray and towel storage space solves the problems.

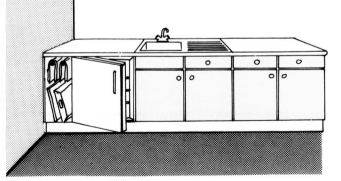

◁ *Tall units* should never be placed in the middle of a run of units as they will interrupt the work suface.

The wall space in between base units and wall cupboards can be lined with narrow shelving, about 4in. deep, or with hooks or pegs for utensils, or with a metal grid storage system.

12"

18"

△ *Wall units* should be positioned about 18in. above the work surface. Any lower and you won't be able to see the back of the work surface without bending down. Any higher, and the top shelves will be difficult to reach.

## WORK SURFACES

The standard height for a work surface is 36in. If you are tall, this may be too low, particularly for the sink, where you work with your hands below the work surface level.

It is worth experimenting to find the height that suits you, but bear in mind that units come in a standard height, which will have to be built up to match unless you can alter the height by adjusting the toekick. Other possibilities include setting special surfaces in the work surface at different heights, such as a butcher's block for chopping or a slab of marble for rolling out pastry.

Work surfaces are generally 25in. deep, but most manufacturers make a deeper one for peninsula units, eating areas or to cover extra-deep appliances.

## APPLIANCES

The appliances you choose will affect the entire kitchen plan, since you will have to place them where they function most efficiently and conveniently for you and everyone else using them. By using existing utility lines, especially the plumbing, you will keep costs down. However, your choices of locations for some units will be limited.

 **Ovens** should be placed at least 12in. away from a corner to allow doors to open easily. Never position an oven within the radius of an inward-opening door. Position an eye-level oven at the end of a run of units, with plenty of work surface to one side for putting down dishes. Watch out for side-hinged doors – the handle should be on the side nearest the work surface.

 **Cooktops** should have at least 12in. of work surface to either side and should never be placed near windows with flapping curtains. Gas cooktops should be positioned out of any drafts in case the burners blow out. Do not place a cooktop under wall units unless you install an exhaust hood.

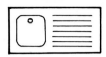 **Sinks** A minimum length of 40in. for sink and draining surface is recommended. The size of sink you need will depend on how big your household is and whether or not you have a dishwasher, but the bowl should be big enough to cope with bulky items such as chopping blocks and pastry boards. Round sinks, although they can be very attractive, are usually impractical in this respect.

If there is enough space, a one-and-a-half or double bowl sink is useful, especially if one of the bowls is fitted with a garbage disposal unit. Allow at least 12in. of work surface or drainer on either side of the bowl for stacking dishes and pans.

**Dishwashers** Best placed as close to the sink as possible for rinsing plates and for convenient water and waste connections. Avoid positioning a dishwasher near a corner as you will need plenty of room to open the door to its full extent for loading and unloading.

 **Refrigerators and freezers** These are usually hinged on the right but some models can be hinged on either side. Allow at least 4in. between the hinge side and an adjoining wall or run of units so that you can open the door wide enough to remove shelves. For tall freezers, an adjacent countertop area of around 12in. is useful.

**Washing machines and dryers** If there is no space for a separate utility room and the washing machine/dryer must be included in the kitchen, it is more hygienic to keep them separate from the food storage and preparation zones. Position the washing machine on the same wall as the sink and/or dishwasher.

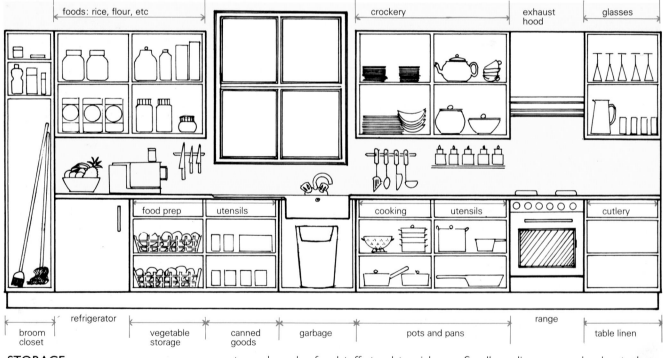

foods: rice, flour, etc | crockery | exhaust hood | glasses

broom closet | refrigerator | vegetable storage | canned goods | garbage | pots and pans | range | table linen

food prep | utensils | cooking | utensils | cutlery

## STORAGE

For greatest efficiency, organize storage around the three zones of the work triangle.

**Food storage** centers around the refrigerator, well out of the way of heat and steam. Use wall cupboards for dry goods such as flour, sugar, cookies, etc. – and store cans and jars of food in cabinets. Keep cleaning materials in a separate cupboard – foodstuffs tend to pick up powerful tastes and smells.

**The preparation area** is near the sink. Keep kitchen knives, strainers, graters, peelers and so on in drawers or hung from racks on the wall, and china and crockery handy for the clean up and serving areas. This is also the place to keep a garbage bin, ideally under or beside the sink.

Small appliances can be kept along the back of the counter or in drawers or pull-out units underneath. Don't keep heavy items in wall units as they are awkward to lift down.

**In the cooking area** you need deep drawers or double floor cupboards for pots and pans, baking dishes and so on, and wall racks and shallow drawers for cooking utensils.

# THE L-SHAPED KITCHEN

## This layout is one of the most functional, giving you a traffic-free zone in which to work.

The L-shape is one of the most versatile kitchen layouts, with its units and appliances ranged along two adjacent sides. It is also one of the most functional because the work triangle isn't interrupted by through traffic.

The L layout is suitable for almost all types of rooms, except narrow ones or those with lots of doors, and is often used to create a kitchen in a corner of an open-plan living room or in an awkwardly shaped corner.

The L is particularly suited to kitchens that incorporate eating areas. It almost always allows space for eating – even if only a breakfast bar – and in most a table can be added comfortably. Not only is it a neat, space-saving arrangement, but it is an extremely sociable set-up, allowing the cook to join in the life of the room – ideal for relaxed informal entertaining and family meals.

### COOKING

The long continuous run of counter space is marvelous for cooking and, when the sides of the L are not too long, this is a very efficient and energy-saving arrangement for the cook.

If one, or both, sides of the L is too long, keep the work triangle compact and use the extra space at the long end for storage of cleaning equipment and materials and for less frequently used cooking utensils and appliances.

Once you have decided on the position of such essentials as refrigerator, cooktop, oven and sink with its attendant plumbing, there are still plenty of ways you can vary, improve and extend the use of the L. Of course, you can choose from dozens of looks.

### Space to work
*A double sink, cooktop, and refrigerator on the far left behind a matching door panel still leave a good stretch of continuous countertop for food preparation. There is plenty of space for two people to work at the same time in this medium-size room and the arrangement allows for a table for informal meals.*

13

**Utensil rack** A towel rack fitted under a wall cupboard and hung with S-shaped hooks provides an attractive and handy place to keep small pots and pans and kitchen tools.

## CHOICES

As well as being extremely practical, the L-shape is a very adaptable arrangement. These three kitchens, for example, are the same size with basically the same layout, but they work in different ways according to the needs and means of their owners.

There are a number of factors that will affect how you organize your kitchen once you've decided on the basic layout and where the appliances should go. You need to consider how much storage you need and where; whether to include an eating area; how many people use the room; what kind of look you want, and so on.

If you are a cook who prefers buying fresh food as you need it, you won't want a lot of storage space for food, or even a very large refrigerator – but you

### Cook's choice

*The three L-shaped kitchens shown here illustrate the variety of uses to which the same basic layout can be put as well as the different looks that can be achieved.*

*The practical laminate kitchen below is designed for a cook who prefers to*

may want extra space for cooking equipment and utensils. On the other hand, you may not have the time or inclination for daily shopping, or perhaps you live in an isolated spot and tend to buy in bulk – in which case you probably want plenty of cupboards and a large refrigerator/freezer.

## BUDGET

Obviously, too, the amount of money available will affect your decisions, but there's no reason why you can't proceed gradually.

Once you've established the work triangle and where to put the sink, range and refrigerator, you can start with a modest set-up of cupboards set under a work surface, replacing old appliances with new, and adding extra floor and wall cupboards as you can.

*have the maximum amount of work surface rather than excess cupboards. A wipeable table provides even more space for food preparation.*

*Floor cupboards are kept down in number with a space left under the countertop by the window for an eating or work area.*

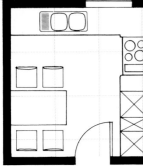

scale: 1 square = 1 square yard

## Floor to ceiling

*These two kitchens are designed for owners prepared to sacrifice a certain amount of counter-top to gain storage space. Both rooms feature cupboards up to the ceiling but that is where the similarity ends.*

*▷ Open shelving and a glass-fronted cupboard contribute to the light, open look of this kitchen.*

*▽ A streamlined kitchen with similar features has been achieved with a totally built-in look.*

## SPOTLIGHT ON CORNERS

Every L-shaped kitchen turns a corner – in the best designed ones, every inch of this space is used to its fullest potential.

Deep corners formed by adjacent units can be a problem but there are now dozens of well-designed corner cupboards available, and almost every manufacturer features at least one kind of carousel or lazy Susan device that fits into a floor corner unit using circular trays or shelves. You can fit wall and floor units with bi-folding doors so that it's easy to reach inside.

A simpler solution is to use open shelving around the corner, at wall or floor level, allowing everything to be seen at a glance.

The corner of the countertop is often a problem area too. It's too deep and awkward to use for work space, but it is an ideal place to keep small appliances when not in use. Another idea is to cut across the corner at an angle and build in a sink or cooktop, or install a built-under oven. This very smart solution allows you additional space at work surface level behind the appliance.

With all these options, there's no reason why the corner of an L-shaped kitchen should be underused.

### ▷ Simple corner

*The corner worktop area is a useful place to keep wooden spoons, spices and the like next to the cooktop. The cupboard underneath houses a swing-out shelf unit. The angled open unit on the wall holds decorative dishes and breaks the solid line of cupboard doors.*

### ▽ Clever corners

*From left to right:*
☐ *A bi-folding door opening out on itself for an unobscured view right to the back.*
☐ *A revolving carousel unit ensures nothing gets lost at the back.*
☐ *A single door with two circular lazy Susan trays that swing out for easy access to small jars and spices.*
☐ *A single cupboard next to a compartment for trays and wine.*

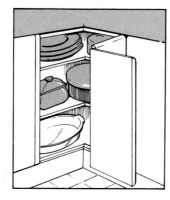
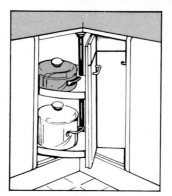

◁ **Sink solution**
The sink, placed across a corner, adds depth to the kitchen and is the perfect peach color to complement the multi-colored granite countertops and gray cabinetry.

Mirrors mounted above the countertops help to create a feeling of space while under-cabinet lighting illuminates the work area. Clean, simple lines and elegant materials, such as the black ceramic floor, combine to set this kitchen apart from the others.

▷ **Corner option**
Fitting a range into the corner is a nice way to use space. The range hood above adds to the simple lines of the cabinet and paneled ceiling. A small storage unit installed above the cooktop provides spices at an arm's reach. Countertops on either side of the range are useful for putting down pots, pans and utensils.

▷ **Using every spare inch**
This tiny room uses the L arrangement to maximum effect and usefulness. All the essentials are neatly incorporated and every bit of space is made to work for its living, with storage cupboards and shelves taken to ceiling height and a sensible amount of cupboard and drawer space. Also, there is just enough room for a small table – both this and the chairs fold up when not in use to give the cook more room to work.

◁ **A family kitchen**
A working kitchen that is also a pleasant place for meals with family and friends. Here the 'business' area is confined to the window recess and along one wall. Elements such as the inlaid vinyl floor and a long cloth on the round table help to define the eating areas and give it a relaxed mood.

▽ **Room to entertain**
A dining area ideal for informal entertaining is created in the opposite corner of this pastel colored, L-shaped kitchen.

# THE U-SHAPED KITCHEN

## This is probably the safest and most efficient of all kitchen layouts, offering maximum storage and workspace.

This arrangement, where units and appliances are placed along three sides of a square or rectangle, is both functional and flexible. There is flexibility in the positioning of countertops and appliances as well as room for plenty of storage, often on at least two complete sides of the U-shape.

Size is less of an obstacle in creating a U-shaped kitchen than awkwardly positioned doorways. In a true U-shaped kitchen no doors break up the line of work surfaces so that the cook is not disturbed by through traffic.

### FIRST CONSIDERATIONS
The U-shape lends itself to the creation of an efficient work triangle whose sides should add up to between 13 and 23ft. Too small a work triangle could feel claustrophobic; an over-long triangle involves extra walking.

**A small kitchen** can accommodate a successful U-shape although it is important to allow space for two people to use the kitchen at the same time – so you need a minimum of about 5-6½ft. of space between the legs of the U-shape.

**Larger kitchens** More people seem to make mistakes with large rooms than with small ones. A spacious U-shape may provide plenty of work surfaces but can give rise to an elongated work triangle; it's best to confine the triangle to the base of the U-shape.

*Through view*
*A U-shaped kitchen, with a full complement of appliances, can be fitted into the smallest of rooms. Space-saving sliding doors and an open pass-through separate this kitchen from the interconnecting living area.*

△ *Room to maneuver*
*This kitchen is wide enough to allow two cooks to work together and open a drawer, cabinet, oven or refrigerator and stand or bend down in front of them without banging into each other.*

*A lot of time in the kitchen is spent at the sink – even if you have a dishwasher. By placing the sink underneath the window, the cook has a pleasant view while working.*

## USING THE SPACE

Careful placement of appliances is important for an efficient and enjoyable layout – and the three-sided U-shape gives ample room for choice.

Plan your layout carefully, using the work triangle principle to find the ideal position for your sink, cooktop and oven, refrigerator and freezer, and other appliances. Apart from considering the work triangle, remember to think about plumbing requirements, access to power, and the need to allow space for doors to open comfortably.

The continuous run of the U-shape means that there is often room for a tall pantry and broom closet. The usual rule applies, however; position them at the end of a run to avoid interrupting the work surface.

It is usually possible to fit in an eating area, even if it is only a bar with stools tucked under it along one leg of the U-shape. If this is separated from the work area by a tall unit, the bar could be at a lower level to suit children or elderly people.

*BRIGHT IDEA*

**Smooth rollers** A pair of special rollers under a slot-in appliance makes cleaning and repairs less of a chore by allowing you to roll the machine forward. The appliance must, of course, have sufficiently long and flexible water and power connections and there must be about 1½-2in. above it for the added height.

◁ **A narrow U-shape**
In a relatively long and narrow room such as this, it's best to confine the work area to the base of the U-shape to avoid time-wasting journeys between the sink, cooktop and food preparation areas.

A work surface should not normally be broken up by tall cupboards or stacked appliances. In this kitchen, the refrigerator and a double oven are positioned at one end of the room, near the door.

▷ **A different arrangement**
This kitchen has been rearranged so that a separate refrigerator and freezer have been tucked under the countertop, replacing the breakfast bar. In addition, the double oven has been replaced by a single oven installed directly under the cooktop. This has freed space for two full-height cupboards, which could act as a broom closet and a pantry.

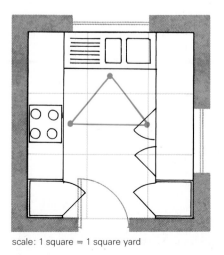

scale: 1 square = 1 square yard

## DIVIDING SPACE

A U-shaped kitchen is not necessarily self-contained. Often, the fourth wall, which would close off the U-shape, is absent, and instead the kitchen interconnects with another room.

Alternatively, a U-shaped kitchen can be linked to another room along one of its legs. Units can run along two walls, with the third leg making a room divider. The floor units that make up the room divider are best fitted with doors that open into both areas, with the countertop providing a convenient serving surface.

The area above the divider units can be left completely open, or open shelving or wall units can partly screen the cooking zone from a dining area. This also allows the cook to keep in touch with what is going on at the table.

▽ ▷ *Double use*
*During the morning, this kitchen opens onto a breakfast area (below). Later in the day (right), the dishes are cleared away and the furniture moved aside to make room for a playpen. This practical arrangement allows a parent to prepare a meal while keeping a watchful eye on a child.*

△ **Breakfast bar**
An extra-wide countertop along one length of the U-shape provides knee room for a breakfast bar.

◁ **Extra storage**
The installation of ceiling-hung units in the kitchen illustrated above greatly increases its storage capacity.

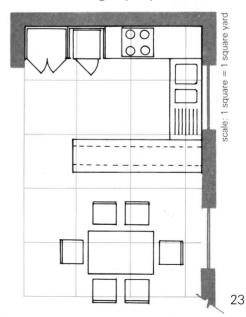

scale: 1 square = 1 square yard

23

## COPING WITH CORNERS

Making the best use of corners can be difficult in any kitchen and with a U-shaped layout you have two to deal with. When planning the basic layout, it is important to ensure that doors do not open into one another and that appliances are positioned at least 12in. from a corner so that doors can be opened fully without banging into the wall.

Most manufacturers include corner units in their product lines – whether carousels for wall or base units or units with bi-fold doors.

### ▷ A corner sink
*An unusual way of making full use of an awkward corner is to install a special sink that cuts across the corner. It's a good idea to install a strip light under the units above the sink.*

### ▽ Soft angles
*Corners can be used to your advantage, as in this semicircular kitchen. By angling the units and a range across the corners, the flow of the work surface is not interrupted. The interesting shape of the angular table adds to the visual interest and provides a working or breakfast table.*

# ONE-WALL KITCHENS

## Compact and easy to run, but often tight on space, single line kitchens need to be planned with ingenuity.

If your kitchen space is limited, a one-wall layout, where units and appliances are arranged along one wall, is often the most efficient arrangement. This layout is equally useful in a multi-purpose kitchen/dining/living room, as units and appliances can be neatly contained in one area, leaving the majority of the floor space free for dining and relaxing.

Cleverly planned, a one-wall kitchen can be as neat and work as well as a minute ship's galley. The road to success lies in allowing as much countertop space as possible, choosing the right units and appliances and having a flexible approach to storage.

## PLANNING THE LAYOUT

The width of the room is a crucial factor in planning. You need 56in. of floor space in order to move around comfortably and open doors.

Start your plan with the sink, which is best positioned in the center of the wall, with the range and refrigerator at either end.

Ideally, there should be counter space between the sink and appliances. If limited space means that this is impossible, place the draining side of

### Single line

*A one-wall layout is a good choice if you want to use the rest of the room for dining. This kitchen, streamlined to perfection, features wooden cabinets with matching dishwasher panel. A white countertop, white knobs and decorative tile add contrast and a personal touch.*

the sink next to the range, so that you have somewhere to put down pans, and choose a refrigerator that slides under the countertop. A slide-in range with a pull-down glass top provides useful extra work space. Both the range and the refrigerator doors should open away from the sink for easy access. Most refrigerators are now sold with interchangeable hinges.

If you have a dishwasher, tuck it underneath the draining side of the sink. This minimizes plumbing costs and means that it is quick and easy to transfer things from the sink to the machine.

Use the remaining space for base units. If possible, incorporate a pantry unit with pull-out wire shelves or a carousel for storing small items. Fit an exhaust fan in the space above the range between wall cupboards. If you have bought units with integral doors (special clip-ons that cover appliances), the exhaust fan can blend into the run of cupboards. If not, look for a pull-out exhaust fan that can be positioned below a wall unit, or a standard exhaust fan above which you can put open shelves or a cut-down cupboard.

A recirculating charcoal filter exhaust unit occupies less space than the ducted type where piping must be run through cupboards to the open air. If you can't afford a fan, leave the space above the oven free, or add a couple of open shelves, starting halfway up the side of adjacent wall cupboards.

If a window interrupts the run, you could incorporate it in the overall design plan by hanging wall cupboards on either side, level with the top of the frame, then join them with a narrow overhead storage shelf. Make sure that wall cupboards allow adequate clearance of the work surface and check that all doors can be opened without banging into each other.

## THE CLASSIC ONE-WALL KITCHEN

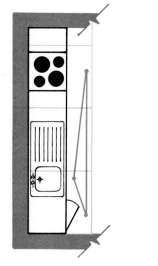

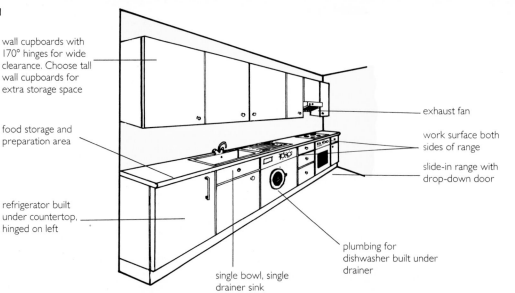

wall cupboards with 170° hinges for wide clearance. Choose tall wall cupboards for extra storage space

food storage and preparation area

refrigerator built under countertop, hinged on left

single bowl, single drainer sink

plumbing for dishwasher built under drainer

exhaust fan

work surface both sides of range

slide-in range with drop-down door

scale: 1 square = 1 square yard

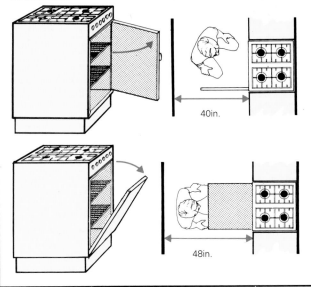

### ▽ Oven door clearance
*Because you can stand at the side of a side-hinged oven door (below) you only need clearance of about 40in. You have to stand directly in front of a flap-down door (bottom), so allow slightly more room – about 48in.*

40in.

48in.

### ◁ Fully integrated
*This one-wall kitchen is part of a larger room; it has been planned to look good as well as work efficiently. The tall unit on the left houses the refrigerator, with two deep drawers underneath and a small cupboard above. The oven is built under the countertop with an inset cooktop above and an integrated pull-out exhaust fan in the wall cupboard.*

### ▽ Built-under bonus
*Planned for maximum counter space, there are no tall cabinets in this alternative version of the same kitchen. The refrigerator, hinged on the left, fits under the countertop. A small cabinet with a work surface on top fits between the range and end wall and is useful for storing pans.*

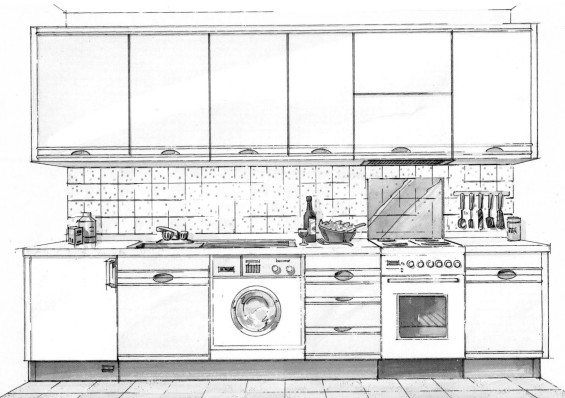

## USING WALL SPACE

The wall facing the main run of units can also be put to good use. Narrow shelves, fitted from floor to ceiling, add invaluable extra storage space. For breakfast or light snacks, attach a hinged shelf to the wall that can be hooked up at mealtimes and folded back down against the wall to keep it out of the way when not in use. Folding chairs can lean or hang beneath the shelf when they are not needed.

## CHOOSING APPLIANCES

In most one-wall kitchens there is not much space for appliances, so shop around for those that will work well in a limited area. Starting with the kitchen sink, there are dozens of shapes and sizes and some of the latest ranges of accessories are designed to make the most of space. Look for chopping boards and drain baskets that fit over the sink. For a neat, streamlined look, go for an inset model in which the drainer is an integral part of the unit and choose a color that matches the surrounding countertop.

If you have a dishwasher, you may be able to do without a drain board. Instead, fit a single inset sink with a drain rack or, if there is room, a pair of inset bowls, one with a garbage disposer.

Modern ranges are neater than the old-fashioned models. Some are designed to match the style of the rest of the kitchen appliances. The new slide-in or drop-in ranges are insulated at the sides and rear so they can fit flush against combustible surfaces. Ranges include gas or electric burners on top and oven/broiler below.

Some microwaves can be mounted between wall units and counters – a great space saver in a one-wall kitchen. A microwave is a useful addition to any kitchen but it should not be seen as a replacement for a conventional oven unless it offers radiant and convected heat as well as microwaves.

▷ *Space at a premium*
*This kitchen is completely functional without being pretentious. Fully equipped with dishwasher, range, microwave oven, refrigerator, and built-in radio/television, the kitchen is ideal for the average cook or gourmet chef.*

*The marble countertop serves as an elegant yet practical setting for the sink with cutting board and wire rinse basket.*

△ *Folding step stool*
*Maximizing storage space in a narrow kitchen often means that some shelves and cupboards are out of reach. Instead of balancing on a chair or ledge, keep a folding step stool handy. It can be hung from a hook on the wall or slipped into a gap between units when folded down after use.*

### ◁ Pull-out pantry

Maximize the potential of cupboards with slide-out shelves. Here a pull-out pantry unit is incorporated into a run of units under the counter. Accessible from both sides, there is room for large bottles at the bottom, while smaller items can be kept in a shallow wire tray at the top.

With minimal cupboard space, storage must be organized efficiently. A small kitchen is no place for clutter, so store little-used items in cupboards, keeping only what's absolutely essential close at hand.

### ▽ Breakfast bar

There is not enough room to fit any cupboards along the right-hand side of this sunny yellow kitchen, which has been brightened up with splashes of green.

Instead, a breakfast bar made from a narrow length of countertop to match the kitchen is attached to the wall by a hinge. This runs along the entire length so that it can be folded down against the wall when not in use.

### ▷ Food center
The food center is installed directly into your countertop for easy-to-clean, high efficiency food processing. The lightweight appliances lock into the power unit and can be stored in a cabinet. An added convenience is the absence of plug-in wires.

### ▽ Vegetable store
The gap at the end of a run of floor units can be left open to hold a plastic-coated wire vegetable rack. With casters it can be easily pulled in and out.

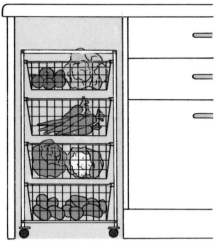

### ▽ Useful space
A small space between wall cupboards can be used for shelves, and a space between base units provides a spot for trays. White walls and units with accessories picked out in a stronger color make a kitchen feel spacious.

## BRIGHT IDEA

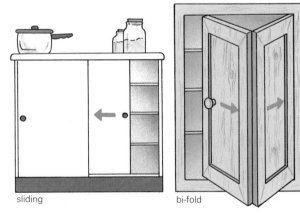

sliding          bi-fold

### SPACE-SAVING DOORS
When it comes to kitchen doors, side-hinged are not the only choice.

**Bi-fold doors**, hinged in the middle, fold back on themselves to allow access to the whole cupboard.

**Sliding doors** take up even less room. Fixed on a pair of parallel runners, one slides alongside the other, giving access to half the cupboard at a time.

Other solutions include tambour doors that slide up and over the top of the cupboard or use roller blinds to cover base units.

# ISLAND KITCHENS

## Best suited to larger rooms, a central island can become the functional heart of the kitchen.

An island kitchen is a U or L-shaped kitchen with an additional 'bit in the middle.' Purists would argue that the island ought to be a permanent and fixed feature but in practice a table or large trolley can serve as an island.

**The work triangle** in an island kitchen can be very compact as the various services can be located close to one another. You can position the range, refrigerator or sink at the island although often the need to bring the necessary services (gas or electricity, and water) from the sides of the room may affect the choice.

**Finding the space** Island kitchens are not suitable for very small rooms. Generally they are spacious, with room all the way around the island to allow cupboard doors both on the island and on the facing run of base units to open easily. A conventional island is about 48×48in. square, and the minimum size is about 24×36in. Too large an island can involve a lot of unnecessary walking, but if the kitchen isn't large enough to accommodate even a small island, it may be possible to enlarge the room, perhaps by combining the kitchen and pantry.

However, an island can often be successfully fitted into a smaller room. Such islands generally serve as countertops only, with no permanent services attached. While a large room can accommodate a standard square or rectangular island, a specially designed curved or irregular-shaped island may be more suitable for a room in which space is scarce.

In addition to the actual surface of the island, it's important to think about the areas above and below. Both can be designed to enhance the 'look' of the room as well as providing useful and accessible storage space. It is also sometimes possible to fit an appliance underneath the island countertop, and a range hood above an island cooktop is extremely useful for removing cooking fumes.

### A classic island

*This beautiful island and breakfast bar is the focal point of the kitchen. Situated in front of the cooktop and oven range, and with its vast countertop space, it is the perfect setting for preparing and serving meals.*

## THE ISLAND WORKTOP

The top of the island can include a cooktop or a sink – or it can serve purely as an extra work surface, perhaps incorporating a breakfast bar.

**Connecting the power** almost always means that the existing floorcovering has to be lifted so that gas, electricity and water pipes and cables can be brought to the island from the sides of the room. So long as a wood floor has sufficient depth below, services can be installed underneath.

Electricity is the simplest service to install, and allows a refrigerator, cooktop,

exhaust fan, and small electrical appliances to be used on the island. In contrast, if you install a sink, it requires both a supply of fresh water and an outlet to remove the waste.

**A simple island** can provide valuable extra working space, perhaps with an inset chopping board or marble surface for rolling out pastry.

Most islands are made to the standard height of 36in. But if you find that this is not always ideal when you are stirring the contents of a casserole or kneading bread, for example, you can install an island at a different height.

△ *A family kitchen*
*Originally, this kitchen was very small – extra space has been created by turning two rooms into one to accommodate an island and a family breakfast bar.*

*The cooktop is located on a side wall, making room on the island for a barbecue grill and a large food preparation area. The space below the countertop houses a refrigerator and a wine rack along with drawers and cupboards.*

32

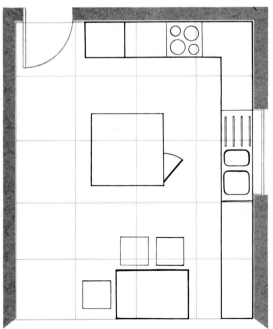

△ **A worktop island**
Providing an island with a gas or electricity supply can be troublesome and expensive, so it's often best to use a new island only as a worktop.

Here, the breakfast bar in the kitchen on the far left has been replaced by a more substantial dining table and the island serves both as a serving area and a working surface. The wine rack below the island is particularly useful for dinner parties.

scale: 1 square = 1 square yard

## BRIGHT IDEA

**A self-opening garbage bin** This ingenious garbage bin is mounted on the inside of a cupboard door so that the lid is opened and closed by a cord when the door is opened or closed.

◁ *Country pine*
*An island need not be custom-built. This pine island has been constructed from four single base units placed back to back and finished off with end panels. The worktop includes a gas cooktop and an electric deep fryer and hot plate.*

▽ *A movable island*
*The trolley in this kitchen makes a movable island, and it is ideal for small as well as more spacious kitchens. The solid maple chopping surface should give years of service, and the vegetable basket, drawer and storage shelf provide a useful place to keep fresh foods and implements. Mounted on four locking casters, the trolley can be moved out of the way when not required.*

# PLANNING A SMALL KITCHEN

## Squeezing equipment, storage and countertops into a small kitchen demands forethought and meticulous planning.

Nowhere is planning more critical than when designing a small kitchen. Squeezing in enough working and storage space can pose a real ingenuity test. While timesaving appliances are essential, they come in set sizes and no amount of wishful thinking can shave off extra inches.

So plan! Start with your priorities. How will you use your kitchen? For quick preparation of mainly packaged meals? Or are you an avid cook who enjoys home-cooked meals? How many people must be cooked for? Is entertaining a priority?

Next, list the appliances and utensils you already own and those you intend to buy. Then stand back and study the space available. Start at the door – get rid of it if you can, or install a sliding door to save vital floor space. Can you remove all or part of a wall so that the kitchen opens into the dining area?

In all probability the majority of kitchen catalogs will set you dreaming but provide little practical help; everything is just a bit too big. You can order specially designed and built units, but this solution is expensive.

So try a different approach. Buy some boating or caravanning magazines and write away for some of the sales literature they offer. You will be surprised at the space-saving ideas featured in their galleys.

From this study you will learn one critical lesson: everything in your small kitchen must have a purpose. There is no room for frills or extras. But that does not mean that it must be a dreary room. Good design and good planning can make the tiniest kitchen a pleasant and attractive room in which to work.

### An open-plan kitchen
*Removing the door into a small kitchen saves space. The entrance to this kitchen, which leads into a dining area, has also been enlarged.*

## STYLE ON A SMALL SCALE

Aim for clean, open lines in your small kitchen so as to create an illusion of greater space. 'Sleek' and 'streamlined' are good descriptions to keep in mind.

Keep colors light: dark wood finishes are fine in a large kitchen but can easily overpower a tiny space. Similarly, decorate the walls to blend rather than contrast with counters and units. The room will appear larger as a result. Integral doors that fit over appliance fronts (except for ranges) are available in most styles.

To prevent blandness, you can highlight the details (such as handles or trims) in contrasting colors.

A fully tiled kitchen is easy to keep clean – an important consideration as walls tend to get dirtier in a confined space. Avoid tiles with strong patterns – instead choose subtle striped effects or gently mottled designs. Rectangular tiles laid widthways across a narrow floor will give the appearance of width.

Use lighting to increase the feeling of space: dark corners crowd in on you. Strong overhead lighting is essential but try to avoid casting harsh shadows. Wall-mounted spotlights concentrate the glow where it is needed and work surfaces can be lit by strip lighting

△ *Sleek and streamlined*
*An all-white color scheme creates clean and simple lines in this narrow, corridor-like kitchen. A spacesaving, baseboard radiator warms the room without disturbing the streamlined effect.*

hidden beneath wall units.

If your list of priorities includes the need for maximum countertop space, covers for the sink and cooktop can add vital work space. Again, such covers will add to the unbroken surfaces in your tiny kitchen, enhancing that all-important feeling of space.

△ **High-tech kitchen**
The use of gray and cool blue combined with silver furnishings and accessories creates a dramatic, industrial effect. This sleek, uncluttered look is fashionable as well as functional, especially for a small kitchen. The sunny windows help keep it from becoming dreary.

▷ **Simple lines**
Finding sufficient storage space is nowhere more important than in a small kitchen. Here, wall units almost to the ceiling make the most of the height of the room, and useful midway units keep spice jars and cooking utensils within easy reach.

## STORAGE AND APPLIANCES

Fitting all the basic equipment into a small kitchen is a problem in itself; finding space for today's timesaving gadgets as well as a well-stocked pantry is a real challenge!

**Appliances and fittings** A sink of practical dimensions is a must. An empty space-saving sink in a showroom or catalog can look capacious, but will it hold even a modest number of pots?

If your small kitchen is a place for the preparation of quick meals you may well want to include a microwave. A combination oven – the latest microwave technology – can function as both a microwave and a normal convection oven.

Refrigerators in small kitchens still need to be roomy enough to store sensible quantities of food. Anything less than 12 cubic feet is probably only sufficient for one person. Carefully loaded, a refrigerator of this size will store a surprising amount of food.

You may have to share your small kitchen with a washing machine. There's little choice in machine sizes, but most models will fit beneath the draining board. A combined washer/dryer saves space. Although a dishwasher will take up valuable space, it is well worthwhile in a small kitchen, providing a place to store dirty dishes.

Timesaving small appliances are always tempting, but they only save time if they are readily at hand. They do occupy valuable counter space, so keep temptation at bay and settle for the essentials: a food processor, coffeemaker and toaster oven.

**Storage** will be a continual problem and every square inch must be utilized. Start by choosing units with pullout racks, carousels and door-mounted storage space. Assess the height of items to be stored in wall units: extra open shelves can almost always be added to increase storage capacity.

Consider a garbage disposer unit in the sink to do away with bulky garbage bins and look, too, at midway units that store spice jars, mugs and other odds and ends.

Hanging utensils on wall-mounted racks in that midway space is another spacesaving idea, leaving cupboards free for less-frequently used items. Ceiling racks are fine if ceilings are high, but they can be dangerous in a room of only average height.

Above all, avoid clutter. Keep only what is absolutely essential near at hand. If you follow this rule your small kitchen will serve you well.

△ **Induction cooktop**
The polished sheen of this precision cooktop enhances the beauty of the finest custom kitchens. With unwavering accuracy, the cooktop responds immediately to the temperature selected on the electronic touch control panel. When the cooktop is turned off, the heating stops instantly.

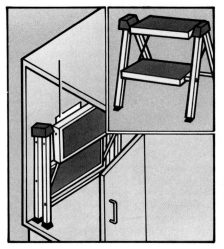

△ **Folding steps**
Steps are essential if the cook is to reach high shelves. These sturdy steps can be stored inside a base unit.

△ **Wall-mounting a microwave oven**
A microwave oven can be hung on the wall at a convenient height (using a specially designed bracket) to free valuable counter space below.

△ **Tidy cutlery**
A two-tier cutlery drawer such as the one shown here keeps cutlery and utensils tidy and gives you twice the storage space in a single drawer.

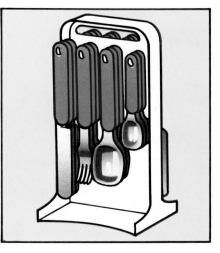

△ **Hanging cutlery**
A cutlery stand can hold a 24-piece cutlery set. Such stands are available in plastic or wood, and the cutlery handles come in various colors.

△ **Multi-purpose sinks**
Kitchen sinks are available in all different shapes, colors and sizes. The corner kitchen sink (left) shown here in sunshine yellow, fits neatly into a

tight corner. The stainless-steel kitchen sink (center) features roomy basins. A sound-absorbing undercoat reduces disposal noise and vibration. The rectangular cast-iron sink, with a rich

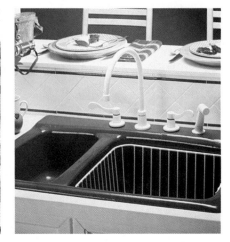

gloss finish shown here in French blue (right), offers an optional hardwood cutting board or coated wire utility basket that can be used as either a colander or plate rack.

△ **Cup hooks**
Cups and mugs are difficult to stack neatly on a shelf – instead, screw a strip of cup hooks or individual hooks under wall units or onto the wall itself.

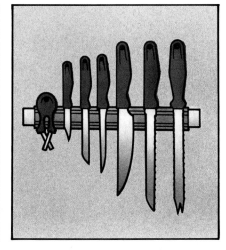

△ **Wall grid**
Made from strong plastic-coated wire, a wall grid fits into the space between wall and base units to keep utensils – even cook books – close at hand.

△ **Magnetic knife rack**
A wall-mounted magnetic strip stores kitchen knives neatly, close at hand and safely out of the way. Knives will stay sharper than if stored in a drawer.

△ **Under-sink storage**
A metal basket that runs on sliding rails attached to the door provides organized storage beneath a sink. Rubber wheels prevent scratching.

△ **A toekick drawer**
This neat, pull-out drawer makes use of the usually dead space in the toekick below base units by providing storage for small, infrequently used items.

△ **Storage behind cupboard doors**
A pegboard attached to the inside of a wall unit door can be used to hang utensils from hooks. In larger spaces, special plastic baskets can be used.

## WAYS WITH DOORS

Hinged doors, by their very nature, take up space when open and in the small kitchen this can be a hazard as well as inconvenient. Dispense with them altogether wherever possible or consider installing sliding or bifold doors.

If you feel you must have a door into the kitchen, try to hinge it so that it opens out of the room. This saves valuable floor space in the kitchen and can prevent an accident if someone enters unexpectedly and bumps into the cook who may be maneuvering hot pans.

A sliding door is a compromise, but the door must still go somewhere and this requires wall space to house it when open. (Sliding doors for base and wall units are also available.) A better choice might be bifold doors, which are hinged down the center. When opened, the door closes back on itself so that it takes up half the space of a standard door.

▽ **Streamlined storage**
*This storage utility with spacious cubby holes and roll out trays, neatly packs away everything from canned goods to napkins and towels.*

△ **A folding division**
*Folding doors can be kept fully closed or open, or partially closed to act as a partition between a small kitchen and a dining area.*

▽ **Bifold cupboard doors**
*Where sliding doors cannot be installed, bifold doors can provide a space-saving solution.*

# KITCHEN STORAGE

One of the secrets of successful storage is to have the right space available for the objects you want to store.

Planning kitchen storage can be difficult. All too often, it's a question of trying to fit a quart into a pint, so start by making a checklist of the items you want to store. This enables you to make the best use of the available space in order to create a tidy, well-ordered kitchen that is a pleasure to use and pleasant to look at.

All in all, there are four basic areas that can provide storage space. Wall cabinets are hung on the walls above work surfaces. The space between these two can be filled with various forms of midway cabinets and shelves. Below the counter, base units contain cupboard and shelf space, often for bulky or heavy items. And finally, don't forget the ceiling. As long as it's high enough, rarely used items can generally find a home here.

As a general rule, frequently used items should be stored close at hand. Things that you rarely use can be stored high up or low down, but avoid keeping bulky or heavy items too high up, too low down, or in very deep cupboards or shelves.

### Combined storage
*In a small kitchen, careful planning of storage is essential if everything is to fit in. Here a combination of cupboards, drawers and open shelves makes use of all the available space. An entire wall with shelves and cup hooks provides a home for decorative and everyday crockery.*

△ *A place for everything*
*This kitchen provides storage space for everything. Underneath the glass cabinets, which supply a perfect place to display pretty china, there is built-in space for the television and computer system. For extra storage space, the island contains drawers as well as a large cabinet.*

## THE RIGHT COMBINATION

Whatever the size of your kitchen, careful planning can help you to find a home for everything. In fact, a huge kitchen isn't necessarily an advantage – think of all the extra miles you would travel during the year! Rather, you should aim to make every single inch of space work to your advantage.

This way, you'll achieve a maximum amount of storage space without creating a cluttered or too functional feel.

Wall and base units are the backbone of most kitchen storage systems. To accommodate pots and pans as well as small dishes, kitchen units should incorporate a mixture of shelves and drawers, both deep and narrow. Adjustable shelves allow you to change the structure of your storage system over time.

**Wall cabinets** Since most people can reach only the first and second shelves in their wall cabinets, use this area to store everyday china and glass or frequently used cans and packages of food.

The higher shelves can hold items used only once or twice a year.

It's best to choose wall units that are slightly shallower than the counter beneath so that you don't hit your head if you lean forward. Cupboards should always be installed over a counter though, and never over an empty space where they could easily be walked into.

Where space is tight, narrow wire shelves can be attached to the back of wall unit doors and used to store small objects. The baskets must be installed so that they slide into the space between the cupboard shelves when the door is closed. High baskets are difficult to reach into, so use only the lower half of the cupboard door.

Leaving some areas open to view makes the contents easy to get hold of but can mean extra dusting.

A grid system along the wall can incorporate such gadgets as a knife rack, somewhere to hang utensils, and perhaps even a useful paper towel holder.

◁ *Drip-dry storage*
The old-fashioned scullery idea of
having a large built-in plate rack so you
just wash them and pop them back
into their drainage/storage place still
has a role to play.

   The drainage area is positioned over
the sink, and is topped and flanked by
open shelving. Cupboards and drawers
below the work surface complete the
storage system.

▽ **The right units**
The storage units in this kitchen are
both practical and decorative. Glass
cabinet doors allow the china and
crystal to be displayed as well as neatly
stored. A large wine rack makes for a
pretty pattern while wall-hung rolls of
wrapping paper and ribbons are a
special convenience. Chilled wine or
other beverages are always at hand in
the two compact refrigerators.

## MIDWAY UNITS

These are designed for the space between countertop and wall units. Most manufacturers offer a range of midways; or you can adapt their ideas.

**Wire grids** are used with butchers' hooks to hang utensils. Some grid systems are enhanced by baskets and shelves. You can make a grid by hanging a wire cake-cooling tray on the wall.

**Hanging rail** A chrome or wooden rail suspended under units can be used to hang utensils, wire baskets, sieves and other odds and ends. Make your own rail from a length of dowel or piping.

**Shelves** Narrow midway shelves are useful for herbs, spices and other frequently used ingredients. Hang cup hooks under the shelves, or buy some slide-on under-shelf containers to make maximum use of space.

**Boxes** Manufacturers offer both open and closed midway storage boxes. Some have interior fixtures, such as plastic compartments for ingredients.

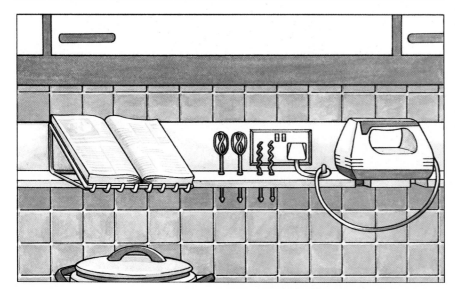

△ *A variety of solutions*
*The planners of this kitchen have incorporated several different types of midway units. Clear plastic storage drawers make it easy to find the right ingredient. Gleaming copper pots hang on a rail above the counter, and knives are always at hand over the chopping block. A wire rack over the sink completes the range of midway units.*

◁ *Adding on*
*Midway units can often be added on to an existing set of wall units. Here, readymade shelves, complete with side brackets, provide a home for condiments, candlesticks and jars. Wooden pegs below can take mugs and cups.*

*Such shelves can be very narrow. A depth of only about 4in. will take mugs and small jars; wider shelves can hold larger items.*

◁ *Custom-built shelves*
*Special-purpose midway storage is relatively easy to construct yourself, although some manufacturers do offer a wide range of units.*

*Here, a midway shelf houses an electric mixer together with its attachments, as well as a useful cookbook holder.*

## BELOW THE COUNTER

Kitchen base units house things of many different shapes and sizes, so it makes sense to have a combination of cupboards, drawers of different depths and open shelves, rather than a uniform row of cupboards and drawers.

**Open shelves** accommodate pots and pans in daily use, and if you have small children who play in the kitchen, a deep open shelf can hold a toy box. A narrow open space can be used to store serving or baking trays, or add a telescopic rod for hanging towels.

**Base cupboards** Pull-out wire baskets mean that you can easily see – and reach – the contents of deep cupboards. There are storage baskets to fit most needs: under-sink baskets, vegetable storage baskets of different sizes, and bottle baskets. Deep shelves are not ideal for base cupboards because objects tend to get pushed to the back.

Corner base units generally incorporate a revolving carousel for storing things in the angle of the corner.

*BRIGHT IDEA*

### BRIDGE IT

Open shelves sandwiched between closed storage look attractive and are handy for frequently used utensils.

Some manufacturers include wire trays instead of solid shelves in their range of options. They are also relatively easy to install yourself using metal oven racks.

◁ **Corner space**
A lazy Susan is the perfect solution for corner storage. Fitting neatly inside a cabinet, the lazy Susan utilizes space to the fullest potential while allowing for a continuous run of cabinets.

△ **Below the plinth**
Enterprising kitchen manufacturers use the plinth space beneath base units as a miniature drawer. It is useful for storing tins, baking trays, shoe cleaning materials or a small 'essentials' toolbox containing, perhaps, spare fuses, a screwdriver and flashlight.

## USING THE CEILING

Don't ignore the ceiling in your search for extra storage space. A hanging rack or rail, or a high shelf, can accommodate a surprising number of pots and pans. Check that it does not interfere with headroom.

◁ *Room at the top*
*Here, utensils not in daily use stand on top of wall units and an extra shelf neatly stores a row of preserve jars. Keep a step stool handy – don't risk standing on chairs.*

▽ *Hanging storage*
*A rack suspended by chains from a crossbeam or joist provides valuable extra storage space. Ready-made racks are available, or you can make your own from lengths of piping or broom handles, and butchers' hooks.*

# LIGHTING THE KITCHEN

## Good lighting can transform a kitchen, making it a safe and pleasant place in which to work.

It's a curious fact that while people often spend considerable sums of money on a new kitchen, the lighting of that newly installed kitchen is often ignored. Yet lighting is possibly more important in a kitchen than elsewhere in the home, partly because of the varied activities that take place there.

Kitchen lighting needs to be conducive to more than just work. The lighting requirements of food preparation differ considerably from those of eating a meal at a kitchen table or breakfast bar. Many families find that their kitchen is the social center of the home, where members of the family gather to chat and exchange news. Since many hours are spent in the kitchen, good overall lighting will do away with the eye strain and headaches that can be caused by time spent in an environment that is too bright or too dim.

Safety should not be ignored. If you work in your own shadow, or in a room where the level of lighting is too low, you are much more likely to suffer an accidental cut or burn.

Finally, there is the question of aesthetics. A beautiful kitchen cannot look its best if the lighting does not do it justice.

### A well-lit kitchen
*Lighting is important in every room, but especially so in the kitchen. This unusual fixture provides overall lighting in an innovative way.*

## LIGHTING THE WHOLE ROOM

Good overall lighting in a kitchen creates the right mood – neither too bright nor too 'atmospheric' – and produces efficient working conditions.

The level of general lighting that should be installed depends on a combination of factors: the strength of the task lighting, the room's aspect, and whether it is decorated in pale or dark colors. Good natural daylight is a great benefit; choose translucent coverings for windows if you need to screen them during the day.

**A central strip light**, though somewhat utilitarian, provides the best light for the least money. Fluorescent strips (even the modern color-corrected types) tend to produce a rather harsh, white light, which has a 'flattening' effect on furniture; incandescent strips give a yellower, warmer light.

**Pendant lights** should not throw a glare into the cook's eyes. Match the fixtures you choose to the style of the room, bearing in mind that simple shapes that won't act as dirt and grease traps are best in a kitchen.

**Spotlights** installed either singly or on a track are flexible as you can angle them more or less where you please. They do create shadows, however, and can cause glare on shiny surfaces.

**Downlights** are neat and inconspicuous, particularly if they are recessed into the ceiling. They direct light downward

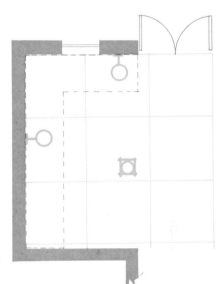

◁ *Classic pendant lighting*
*A series of pendant lamps installed with classically simple shades provide illumination for the whole room and specific task lighting over the counters. Such lights must be carefully positioned: if these lamps were any lower, the cook would be forced to work in a disturbing glare.*

*The single spotlight requires a crown-silvered bulb to reduce glare; it is angled to direct light onto the movable trolley.*

▽ *Uplighting the kitchen*
*A pair of elegant halogen uplights direct their beams onto the ceiling and bounce light back into the room. Uplights work on the principle of reflected light, so the ceiling must be white or at least pale. Dimmer switches control the light level.*

*The cart is lit by a halogen downlight. The fitting that has been chosen incorporates a swivel movement allowing the direction of the light to be altered.*

scale: 1 square = 1 square yard

with a broad or narrow beam, depending on the fixture chosen; some types can be angled.

**Wall lights** that bounce light off a pale ceiling provide overall illumination and help to avoid shadows. Although halogen fixtures are expensive, the quality of the light they produce is excellent. Since the fixtures take very high wattage bulbs, only one or two halogen uplights will be needed to light an entire kitchen.

**Concealed strip lighting** can be installed below wall units or open shelves so that the light, but not the light fixture, is visible. Installing such fixtures is one of the easiest ways of improving kitchen lighting. (Either make a baffle to conceal the light or buy one from kitchen specialists.) Fluorescent strips can cast very white light; incandescent strips give a warmer and yellower light.

△ *A hand-painted kitchen*
*The lighting in this custom-made kitchen, hand painted in shades of old rose, shows off its delicate lines and glowing colors.*

*Concealed incandescent strip lighting below the wall units provides task lighting and casts a warm, yellowish glow. (Some fluorescent strips give off a colder, whiter light and would make the delicate pink appear bluer in color.) Recessed downlights installed in the ceiling provide inconspicuous overall lighting; the gold-effect reflectors enhance the warm quality of the light.*

▷ *Varied lighting*
*A combination of fluorescent strips and downlights light this all-white kitchen.*

*Fitted both below and above the wall units, fluorescent strips throw a white light down onto the work surfaces (including the sink) and upward on to the ceiling. The ribbon of light around the top of the room that the strips create adds a definite touch of drama. The recessed incandescent downlight lights the rest of the room.*

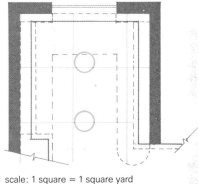

◁ **Modern and streamlined**
*Concealed strip lighting above and below the wall units casts a yellowish glow onto counters and ceiling, balancing the cool color of the kitchen units. The miniature eyeball-type, recessed downlights sparkle and glitter, but leave the floor in relative darkness. Neither the hidden strips nor the downlights disturb the streamlined look of the room.*

## TASK LIGHTING

Efficient kitchen lighting must be shadow-free. This means that any task lighting you install must be positioned so that you do not stand between the light source and the counter. Beware, also, of the glare that can be caused by bouncing over-bright light off shiny tiles, countertops and appliances. Either direct the light away from reflective surfaces, or use lower wattage bulbs.

So long as there are wall units (or shelves) above the counters, the best way of providing task lighting is to install strip lights underneath. But if your kitchen has no built-in wall cabinets, suspend a number of pendant lamps over the counters. Positioning them above the outside edge of the counter will ensure that you cast no shadow as you work. Alternatively, one or more angled work lamps on a shelf or the counter itself provides adequate task lighting.

Even if the sink is located beneath a window, it will need its own light source. A downlight on the ceiling should do the job well (it's best to avoid spotlights since they produce a very strong, glaring light). Another alternative is to install hidden lighting behind a valance. Similarly, the cooktop needs a separate light source. Many range hoods incorporate an integral light; if you need to install a light, choose a fixture in which the bulb or strip is enclosed to protect it from heat and grease splashes.

▽ **Alternative arrangement**
*The two large recessed downlights that replace miniature eyeballs in this lighting scheme ensure that light reaches the rather dark floor. They throw a wide beam and create two overlapping pools of light.*

*An additional strip light installed below the display shelves highlights the collection of ornaments. It has been hidden behind a baffle (painted to match the walls) for safety as well as style.*

scale: 1 square = 1 square yard

## LIGHTING A DINING AREA

The lighting in a kitchen that includes a dining area must be flexible enough to create the right atmosphere for meals.

The simplest arrangement is to make sure that one of the light fixtures used for general illumination is positioned above the table. A pendant lamp will emphasize the eating area, and the type of fixture you choose will set the style of the dining area.

It's best to arrange for the dining table lighting to be switched independently or to have a dimmer switch installed so that the overall lighting level, particularly in the kitchen area, can be reduced at mealtimes.

▷ *Farmhouse style*
*An elaborate pendant lamp, in the style of an oil-lamp, turns this dining table into the room's focal point. The remainder of the lighting is provided by inconspicuous recessed downlights and under-cupboard incandescent strips.*

▽ *A kitchen/diner*
*A modern pendant lamp highlights the dining table in a large kitchen and yet remains in keeping with the style of the rest of the lighting. The lamp is suspended from a rise-and-fall fixture so that it can be lowered for formal meals and raised for family dinners.*

# COUNTERTOPS AND BACKSPLASHES
## Your choice of kitchen worktop should combine practicality with good looks.

Since kitchen counters have to bear the brunt of most cooking activity, they must be able to withstand the heavy wear and tear that they will be subjected to without becoming worn or grubby. Although backsplashes don't need to be quite so hardwearing, they should nevertheless be easy to clean.

Even if you always use a chopping board, a counter will occasionally be subjected to nicks and scratches. So the surface must be strong and resilient. It also must be able to withstand at least moderate heat to prevent burn marks if a hot pan is put down on it. And since you are bound to spill things on it, the ideal worktop is also easy to clean, stain-resistant and waterproof.

Lastly, counters and backsplashes should be as attractive as possible since they are an important element in any kitchen design.

**The dimensions** Standard base units are 36in. in height since this is judged to be the most comfortable height for most people. But if you are taller or shorter than average, some kitchen manufacturers can alter the height of the toe kick in order to raise or lower the counter accordingly.

The normal depth of base units (from front to back) is 24in. and the worktop is usually a few inches deeper. It is possible to install a deeper counter by positioning base units a small distance from the wall. This gives more room to arrange toasters, coffeemakers and similar appliances neatly along the back wall without encroaching on work space — and also means that pipes can be hidden behind the units.

**Materials** Kitchen countertops can be made from many different materials, with differing visual and practical characteristics and, of course, different prices. The most common materials are plastic laminates, wood and ceramic tiles. Granite, marble and man-made materials that resemble natural stone are also available.

### Farmhouse style
*Wooden countertops and a tiled backsplash provide practical surfaces in keeping with the natural style of this kitchen. A butcher's block acts as a chopping board and a marble slab on top of the counter provides a cool surface for rolling out pastry.*

## PLASTIC LAMINATES

By far the most popular choice for kitchen countertops, plastic laminates are available in an overwhelming variety of colors and effects. These range from pale pastels to bright primaries, through imitations of natural materials such as wood and marble – even bold geometric patterns.

A plastic laminate is made up of a thin sheet of plastic bonded to chipboard, blockboard or plywood (in ascending order of quality and price). Formica is the brand name of one of the best known ranges of plastic laminates. Melamine is a cheaper alternative to plastic laminate and is made from plastic-impregnated paper.

Laminate can be bought separately in cut lengths for DIY kitchen assembly, or to replace an existing countertop.

Although boiling water and hot splashes will do no harm, a hot pan or iron should never be placed directly on a laminate counter. Similarly, laminates are generally resistant to knocks and scratches, but should never be used as a chopping surface.

△ *Sleek laminate*
*Curved white laminate cabinets create a modern feel that boasts form and function. To match the sleek design, recessed lights are strategically placed. Solid surface countertops and built-in appliances complete this luxury kitchen.*

▽ *Many choices*
*The plastic laminate counters shown below – speckled gray, plain pink and wood-effect – are just three of the huge variety available. The edge of the counter may be square (in this case cleverly accentuated with a darker pink inset stripe) or curved.*

## CERAMIC AND QUARRY TILES

While most ordinary ceramic tiles can be used for kitchen counters, tiles manufactured specially for this purpose will last longer. Quarry tiles, designed to be laid on floors, are also suitable and create a rugged, rustic feel. Although countertop and quarry tiles are thicker than ordinary ceramic wall tiles, they can be attached to walls to create a coordinated backsplash.

Look for ranges which include curved edging tiles for a neat finish. (Some manufacturers even produce mitered edging tiles for the corners.) Alternatively, a wooden edging will neatly frame countertop tiling.

Tiles are very easy to keep clean, are not easily scratched and are less likely to be damaged by hot saucepans than many other surface materials.

A tiled counter is noisy to work on. In addition, individual tiles can be chipped or cracked if something heavy is accidentally dropped, though this is less likely to happen with quarry or purpose-made tiles. Replacing a single tile can be difficult.

Tiles can be laid over an existing – perhaps disfigured – counter but it is important to ensure that the existing worktop is strong enough to take the weight of the tiles. If it is not adequately supported, a tiled counter can begin to sag.

**Grouting** Since the tiles on a counter are laid on a horizontal rather than a vertical surface, water is liable to collect on the surface, particularly in the grouting, which is usually slightly recessed. This means that waterproof grouting is essential to prevent water seeping into the surface below the tiles. It is also important to ensure that there are no gaps between the tiles and the grouting, where crumbs and similar bits could collect.

Grouting can, with time, get very grubby and needs to be regularly cleaned with a stiff brush and a solution of domestic bleach. It may occasionally be necessary to rake out the existing grouting and replace it. However, there are epoxy grouts available on the market that will not deteriorate. Ask about them when you shop for tile.

## MAN-MADE STONE

Although the various synthetic materials now available for kitchen countertops feel like smooth stone and can look like marble or granite, they suffer from none of their disadvantages (except price). Corian (the best-known man-made stone) is virtually indestructible – it is hardwearing, warm to the touch and completely heat and stain resistant. Small scratches are easily removed by rubbing down with ordinary kitchen cleaner. It can be molded into almost any shape, to create an integral counter, sink and draining board with no joins in which dirt and germs can hide. However, it is more expensive than laminate.

▽ *Shades of pink*
*A tiled counter and backsplash add color and interest to this all-white kitchen. The large expanse of tiles is broken up by mixing various shades of pink on the counter and combining white and pink tiles and a border with a fuchsia design on the backsplash. Gray grouting complements the pink tiles and won't become discolored.*

## WOOD, GRANITE AND MARBLE

These natural materials all produce elegant and attractive, though expensive countertops.

**Wood** A wooden counter is best made from a hardwood – teak, maple, oak and beech are common choices. Some are sealed with a clear varnish; others are treated with a special oil that must be periodically renewed. The types of wood used for countertops is hardwearing and will withstand moderate heat although very hot pans may scorch the surface. A tiled inset next to a cooktop or oven can be used for hot pans.

Solid wood comes in different thicknesses (and therefore different qualities); wood veneer (where a thin sheet of real wood is bonded to chipboard or hardboard) represents a cheaper alternative.

**Marble and granite** are undoubtedly elegant and virtually indestructible – but are also very expensive and heavy, so units (and the floor) may need to be reinforced in order to be able to bear the weight. Marble is porous and should be coated with a special sealant to help prevent staining. Granite is less porous and also comes as a veneer.

△ *Granite splendor*
*There is no arguing with the fact that the granite counter and backsplash add a touch of opulence to this kitchen. The shiny, mottled gray surface goes well with bright primary colors. Granite comes in a variety of colors that include dark and light grays as well as shades of green and pink. While some granites are very mottled, in others the color is more solid.*

◁ *A maple countertop*
*Tough enough to be used for squash courts and dance floors, solid maple is an ideal choice for a counter. Treated with respect, wood actually improves with age and use, unlike plastic laminate or tiles.*

*A custom-made wood counter can replace an existing damaged one – or add the finishing touch to a new kitchen. The counter's edge can be square, rounded or even chamfered – depending on your preference.*

## BACKSPLASHES

As the name implies the backsplash area above the counter must be easy to clean so that splashes and spills from cooking can be removed without causing lasting damage.

The choice of material depends partly on your choice of countertop and kitchen cabinets. Ceramic wall or countertop tiles, quarry tiles, laminates – even marble and granite – are all suitable.

In addition, of course, a backsplash can be painted or covered with wallcovering. Although it is fairly easy to renew paint and wallcovering, it's best to use an oil-based paint or a washable cover to give a reasonably longlasting finish. Instead of tiles, consider a tile-effect washable wallcovering that looks very much like real tiles.

Visually, the counter and backsplash should not be equally dominant or the end result could be overwhelming. A bright or highly patterned backsplash is best combined with a plain or pale counter, and vice versa. Remember too that strong patterns – on either the counter or the backsplash – may conflict with the many utensils that find a home on most kitchen counters, thus creating a working environment that is too busy and distracting.

△ **A personal backsplash**
In a farmhouse-style kitchen, a fully tiled backsplash may look out of place. Here, a small tiled area of Victorian tiles framed in wood, provides a practical and sympathetic backdrop to an old, marble-topped sideboard.

Odd tiles, as opposed to a complete set in the same pattern, are easy to find in antique shops and markets. Choose tiles that have a theme – or a color – in common.

▷ **Checkerboard effect**
Combined with plain units and countertops, an eye-catching backsplash can form the visual focus of a kitchen.

Here, a simple arrangement of black and white tiles is reminiscent of the op art so popular during the 1960s.

A softer effect could be produced by using more subdued colors or patterned tiles.

**A pull-out table** can fit snugly into a drawer space and slide out to extend the available counter space. Such an extendable surface could also double as a tea tray or occasional breakfast table.

When you choose a pull-out table, check that it is securely supported along its entire length when extended.

## MAKING COUNTERTOP SPACE

Except for those lucky enough to possess an exceptionally large kitchen, most cooks would agree that they have insufficient counter space for their needs. The most costly solution is to completely rearrange the entire room in order to squeeze in as much counter space as possible. But there are less drastic solutions.

Start by trying to free as much of the existing space as possible. Rows of storage jars or tins may look attractive ranged along the back wall, but they do take up valuable space. Small appliances such as food processors can often be stored in cupboards rather than on the counter. Some kitchen manufacturers even offer pull-out shelves that allow appliances to be stored behind closed doors.

If there is room, a movable trolley can serve as an additional counter (as well as providing extra storage) – but choose a version with locking wheels for safety. You may even be able to purchase an old butcher's block with a solid wood top that makes an ideal chopping board.

△ *A movable trolley*
*A trolley with locking casters provides an extra counter that can be moved out of the way when not in use.*

▽ *Table storage*
*A roll-out table is convenient when you need added counter space or a quick and easy dining arrangement.*

# COLOR IN THE KITCHEN

## The color scheme you choose plays an important part in bringing the right atmosphere to your kitchen.

Creating a pleasing color scheme for a kitchen can be more complicated than for any other room in the home because there are so many elements to consider. Kitchens generally contain expensive appliances and built-in units that cannot be replaced at a whim.

Built-in units come in a whole host of colors and finishes, ranging from the highly dramatic to the subtle. Since colored facing panels are now available for many kitchen appliances, a degree of color coordination can be achieved between appliances and units as well as surfaces such as walls and ceiling.

Kitchens contain, too, many small appliances and utensils that are always on show. If too many colors or patterns are involved, the result is busy and tiring on the eye.

The room's size and aspect always influence the colors chosen. A small, dark room benefits from light, airy colors and – in addition – the smaller the room, the greater the risk of fragmentation; so use plain, uninterrupted colors for a stream-lined look.

These are just some of the considerations to bear in mind when planning your kitchen. Choose colors and patterns for the long term and – as you decide on the main colors – remember to consider the accessories that will add the finishing touches.

### Fresh and simple
*The color of the wooden units in this kitchen is lifted by the crisp white contrast and a judicious use of clear primaries. The use of lime green gives the room extra zest.*

## LARGE AREAS OF COLOR

When choosing the main colors or patterns that will predominate in your kitchen, it's a good idea to start with the built-in units and countertops. Then consider the elements that can be changed more easily and cheaply – wall and floorcoverings, or paint (and, of course, the accessories and details).

Apart from your personal preferences and the mood you're aiming for, be sure you can live with your choice over the years. A good choice, for instance, is built-in cabinets in neutral white, beiges and creams, or natural wood.

The amount of daylight is an important consideration. Pale colors reflect light and can make a room feel larger, but too much white could be dazzling in a sunny, south-facing kitchen.

▷ *Formal stripes*
*Strong patterns don't look their best broken up by shelves or racks, so keep them away from work areas – like this striped wallpaper above the wall units.*

▽ *Colored units*
*Moss green kitchen units create a restrained background in this room. Custom-stained flooring, a rug and matching seating complete the look.*

△ **Strong color**
The bold colors of this kitchen define it as clearly contemporary. Cabinet surfaces, refrigerator, dishwasher, trash compactor and both islands feature an out-of-the-ordinary dark jade. The island topped with a white counter provides for a contrast in color. The touches of red help to brighten this darker color scheme.

◁ **High-tech look**
Glossy black kitchen units create a streamlined, modern look, with the pale wood trim on the units adding a subtle note of relief to the stark black. Neutral walls and counters, together with a black floor, complete the overall scheme.

## COLOR IN THE DETAILS

The kitchen, with small counter appliances, utensils, storage pots and jars, table linen and crockery, affords great scope for using small areas of color to highlight and break up the large expanses of countertops and units. Planning is important, however, both to stop the room from becoming too busy and to prevent colorful accessories' clashing with each other.

Having decided on the main colors for the room, choose accessories that blend or contrast with the overall scheme. If the background is pale and unobtrusive so that the main color interest lies in the accessories, try to select at least a couple of larger items in the accent color of your choice – tiles, perhaps, or the tablecloth or window covering.

Then color match the rest of the room's details as far as possible to avoid a fragmented look. Paint door and window frames to blend with the color scheme. Although it may be difficult to find small electrical appliances in identical colors, you should be able to find complementary shades or discreet neutrals. Light fixtures, pots and pans, chopping boards, oven gloves, hand towels, mugs, the cutlery and crockery – even the kitchen sink – can all add to your color scheme.

△ ◁ *A whole new look*
*The two kitchens shown here (above and left) are structurally identical, and have the same layout, built-in units and dining table. The difference lies in the clever use of colored detailing that transforms the look of the room.*

*The kitchen above is enlivened by using plenty of red and white – from the wallpaper to the floor and a range of accessories.*

*In the kitchen on the left, a soft and sophisticated color scheme has been created by retaining the same units and combining them with delicate pastel shades throughout.*

▷ *Bold primaries*
*Many kitchen appliances and accessories are available in a variety of colors. In this kitchen a basic black and white look is enhanced with bright red pieces: the garbage pail, a shiny sink, even the napkins. It all adds up to a cosmopolitan look.*

BRIGHT IDEA

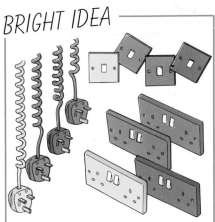

**Electrical fixtures** come in many bright colors as well as standard white, and so can be used to enhance any style or color scheme. They are also available in other materials and finishes such as brass and chrome.

◁ *Blue outline*
*A simple off-white color scheme is given a smart new look with light blue walls and ceiling and an unusual latticework. This is repeated on the countertop, backsplashes and tiled floor.*

◁ *Painted details*
Even a small amount of decorative stenciling can add color and a personal touch. The painted ribbons and flowers give a country feel to this cozy kitchen. A blue and white checked rug adds warmth to the wooden floor while recessed lights provide unobtrusive, uncluttered lighting.

▽ *A painted kitchen*
In a kitchen that lacks built-in wall cabinets, it is easy to introduce color by painting the walls. Do beware, though, of creating an overpowering atmosphere if you opt for a strong color. Here, for example, touches of red and brown break up the large expanses of green and tie in well with the cherry motif on the curtains.

# STREAMLINING KITCHEN SPACES

Gaps between units and appliances can be filled to give your kitchen a built-in look.

## REMODELING ON A BUDGET

Problem When installing a built-in kitchen, a limited budget can make it impossible to afford the number of base units needed. How can the kitchen be made to look built-in and streamlined without filling all the space with expensive units?

Solution Use a combination of built-in units and open shelves. Space the closed units to suit your needs, then fill up the spaces in between with inexpensive shelving. Laminated shelving comes in white, wood effect, primary and pastel colors.

You can even leave some gaps the width of a standard base cabinet. This allows you to insert a unit when you can afford it.

Open shelves between units can be used in many different ways. Two deep shelves provide room for a wine rack. Wire or wicker baskets can be used on narrow shelves for convenient and easily accessible storage. You may require space for a computer or a communication center. A simple desk or shelf space will do.

## SPACE FOR TOWELS OR TRAYS

Problem What can be done with a narrow space too small for a kitchen unit?

Solution Gaps, at the end of kitchen units, or between them on a wall, that are the wrong length to accommodate an exact number of standard units are irritating and a waste of space.

Use the gap to house trays, or buy a custom-made unit to fill the space.

A most useful accessory is a telescopic towel rack. These are available with two or three arms. The rack can be placed beneath the work surface above the gap, on the back wall. The rods pull forward so that towels are easy to reach.

Another way to fill the space is to buy a set of folding kitchen steps. These measure around 3½in. wide when folded and will slide into a narrow under-counter space. It is also possible to buy steps that fit behind a removable section of the base plinth.

Alternatively, hang shelves across the gap and use them to store small jars of spices and other odds and ends.

△ *Adding an eating area*
*A simple breakfast bar can be used to fill space between units or across the end of the room. A length of counter-top makes a good, solid top.*

## ADD A BREAKFAST BAR

Problem What is the best way to deal with a long gap if you can't afford to fit units?

Solution Run a countertop or a narrow shelf across the gap and add a couple of stools to create an instant breakfast bar. If you want to make use of the space beneath the counter, fill it with wine racks (available made-to-measure from some wine and liquor stores), stacking plastic boxes or tiers of wire trays on casters.

You can link units across the end wall of a room by running a narrow breakfast bar between them. This works particularly well if the bar can be positioned beneath a window. Eating breakfast or a snack facing a blank wall is less appealing. The area beneath the bar must be left open so that the cabinet doors can be used.

◁ *Using open spaces*
*The look of country traditions combines an arched valance with custom cutouts for open shelves and alcoves. Glass door inserts, tamboured storage and under-cabinet drawers provide unique design options.*

65

### ◁ Filling the gaps
*Gaps beside a range or between units can be filled with a useful telescopic towel rack.*

## GAPS AROUND THE RANGE
<u>Problem</u> Old ranges were not designed to fit in with modern kitchen units, so there are often narrow gaps at each side. How can these gaps be filled to give a neat, streamlined look?
<u>Solution</u> Gaps beside the range are a collecting point for crumbs and food spills. You can fill the space with a piece of countertop, mounted on a furring strip at one side (the furring strip can be fixed to the wall or unit next to the gap) and flush against the side of the range at the other side. This stops anything from falling into the gap.

The space below the counter can be used as a tray recess, for a telescopic towel rack, or filled with shelves for storing spices and other ingredients.

## SPACE BETWEEN WALL UNITS
<u>Problem</u> Where a kitchen has been fitted in a haphazard way, with cabinets at different levels and spaces between them, the effect is visually disturbing and untidy. How can this broken arrangement be given a neat, streamlined look, without fitting a completely new range of cabinets?
<u>Solution</u> Where there are several cabinets mounted at different levels, the easiest way to bring them together is to run a shelf across the top. The

### ▽ Space between units
*Spaces between both wall and floor cabinets can be filled with open shelves set at different depths. Use shallow baskets on the shelves to keep small items in order and easily accessible.*

### △ Around the range
*Narrow spaces around and above this range have been filled with open shelving to give a streamlined look.*

shelf should be positioned just above the highest unit. Use the shelf to display an attractive collection of jugs, pots or bowls and you'll draw the eye away from the cabinets. Run a second shelf across the bottom, starting beneath the lowest unit. Running shelves across top and bottom creates interesting spaces that can be used for display. You can attach cup hooks to the underside of the bottom shelf and use them for hanging mugs or utensils.

Wall cabinets can be linked by running open shelves between them. Space shelves wide apart for pans and other large objects, close together for spice jars and odds and ends.

## LINING UP NEATLY
<u>Problem</u> Too many appliances can crowd the countertop. Often the appliances are all different shapes and sizes, which results in a messy look.
<u>Solution</u> One of the most convenient ways to deal with this problem is to install under-the-counter appliances. That way, each appliance will have its own permanent position above the countertop. This frees up much needed counter space.

Another way to deal with this problem, as shown on page 30, is a food center unit. With the food center, appliances can be stored away, and only one power unit, built into the countertop, is needed to operate a variety of appliances.

## MIDWAY STORAGE
<u>Problem</u> In a kitchen where storage space is limited, it seems wasteful not to use the area between the countertop and the cabinets. What kind of attachment can be used here without obstructing the counter space?
<u>Solution</u> Fitting baskets to the underside of wall cabinets doesn't obstruct the space below. Under-shelf baskets are available made from plastic-covered wire mesh with open fronts, or from rigid plastic with up-and-over doors. The up-and-over door type is useful for storing bread, biscuits and other perishables.

Cup hooks hung beneath units are useful for hanging mugs and bunches of dried herbs. If your greatest need is for hanging storage, attach metal mesh grids to the wall between the cabinets and the counter. Use butchers' hooks to hang utensils from the racks. Some racks feature a range of accessories, such as hook-on baskets for cleaning materials, shelves and a circular container to hold soap. These are useful above the sink.

Narrow shelves are another way to use the wall space. The shelves should be a maximum of 6in. wide and must finish at least 10in. above the counter. Shelves wider or lower than this obstruct the countertop. Use the shelves for spice jars and other small containers.

# BASIC BUILT-IN KITCHEN UNITS

## The right combination of units is the key to a successful kitchen.

A built-in kitchen means that all or nearly all available space is used for storage, with no obvious gaps between units. A fully built-in kitchen consists of matching wall and floor cabinets that incorporate a sink, oven, dishwasher and continuous countertop.

Cabinets go a long way toward defining the style of a kitchen, and they must be durable enough to withstand thousands of openings and closings, loadings and unloadings over years of use.

**Stock versus custom cabinets** Stock cabinets are, literally, in stock wherever they are sold. They are made in a wide variety of standard sizes that you can assemble to suit your kitchen space.

In general, cabinets are available in two versions, upper and lower units. The uppers are usually 12in. deep and anywhere from 12in. to 36in. in length. Some older uppers were built as large as 5ft. tall. Lowers are usually 20in. to 24in. deep and 32in. to 36in. off the floor. The actual heights and sizes depend upon the size and needs of the user and any local code requirements.

Materials used to make cabinets include solid wood (hard or soft), wood and particleboard, or wood and hardboard. They may be carefully jointed and doweled, or they may be merely nailed and glued together. Depending on the quality, stock cabinets range in price from inexpensive to moderately costly.

A modest amount of money can be saved by purchasing unfinished stock cabinets and then staining or painting them yourself. A bit more can be saved by purchasing knockdown cabinets, which are shipped flat to lower the costs of packing and delivery. Knockdowns are sometimes unfinished.

On the other hand, custom cabinets are priced moderately to very costly. Because custom cabinets are made to order, delivery may take from 4 to 16 weeks. Be sure to place your order well in advance of the date you will need the cabinets. Although some stock cabinets need to be finished yourself, custom cabinets are delivered fully finished.

**Tall units** These cabinets stand on the floor, and are designed to be used as broom closets, pantries or for housing appliances, especially split-level ovens. A typical tall unit suitable as pantry/broom closet or for housing an oven stands around 80in. high (24in. wide, 24in. deep).

**Wall units** should be attached to the wall above the counter and are generally around half the depth of base units so you don't hit your head on them when using the work surface below. Before buying wall units decide whether you want them to go right up to the ceiling – taller cabinets are usually more expensive, whereas standard units may leave you with wasted space above.

If you have tall cabinets in your kitchen, standard wall units are generally positioned so that all the tops line up. If there are no tall cupboards, you need a gap of about 18in. between the top of the countertop and the bottom of the wall units – for practicality's sake.

**Materials** There is a wide choice of materials for kitchen units. Generally, the frames and shelves of cabinets are made from chipboard faced with melamine. Doors and drawer fronts (fascias) and sometimes the exposed end panels are made of other decorative materials:
☐ Solid wood (pine, oak, birch, cherry, maple, pecan).
☐ Wood veneer (thin wood strips glued to chipboard – less expensive than solid wood, but similar in finished appearance).
☐ Wood/plastic laminate mixture (white, colored or textured melamine laminate, wood trims and handles).
☐ Plastic laminate (white or colored, plain, textured or wood-effect) such as melamine or the popular brand Formica. There are also lacquer, polyester and other special finishes.

**Countertops** Chipboard faced with plastic laminate is the most popular choice, but other options include hardwood, ceramic tiles, quarry tiles, granite, marble, or a solid man-made stone-like material such as Corian.

## BASE UNITS

   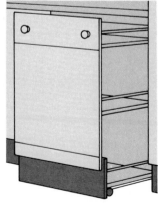

**STANDARD CABINETS**
**Style** Floorstanding cupboards with one, two or three doors depending on the width of the unit.
**In use** Base units come in two styles – plain and with drawerline. Plain units have full-height doors; drawerline units have drawers at the top. Single unit doors can be hinged on the left or the right.
**Watchpoint** High-quality units offer a choice of shelf positions, unit bottoms are coated with a sealant to prevent moisture swelling the chipboard, adjustable feet keep the frame off the floor and there are additional supports in the center of long shelves.

**DRAWER UNITS**
**Style** Available in the same sizes as standard units, drawer units consist entirely of drawers.
**In use** A good number of drawers in a kitchen is useful and a drawer unit should always be incorporated especially if plain – no drawerline – base units are used. Most drawer units have three or four drawers: pan drawers have two deep drawers – the whole unit including drawers, fascia, and sometimes the plinth fascia too, pulls out for maximum access – particularly suited for storing saucepans.
**Watchpoint** Check that the drawers open and close smoothly.

67

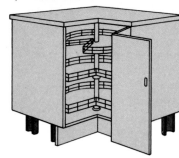

L-shaped corner unit

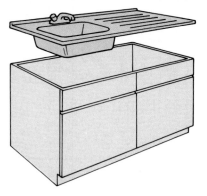

Straight corner unit

## CORNER UNITS

**Style** A base unit that is designed to fit into a corner between two meeting runs of units.

**In use** There are two types of corner units. The L-shaped corner unit has open shelves or a double-hinged door so that the entire contents of the shelves can be seen.

Often enhanced with swing-out shelves. Alternatively there is a straight corner unit. This is a double unit with only one door – the other half of the unit is just open shelves. The adjacent units then fit against the open half. With the shelf removed, this type often has a built-in carousel (see opposite).

## SINK UNITS

**Style** A unit for a kitchen sink.

**In use** Sit-on sink/drainers (usually stainless steel) are designed to sit directly on one of these units. Such a sink also incorporates a lip that runs along the front of the unit and

a narrow 'backsplash' along the back. A sink unit usually doesn't have a central shelf, as the space is needed for the plumbing. A drawerline sink unit has only one real drawer under the drainer, plus a dummy drawer in front.

# TALL UNITS

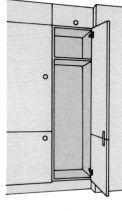

Pull-out larder unit

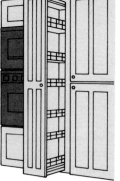

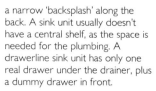

## BROOM CLOSETS

**Style** A tall cupboard for storing cleaning equipment

**In use** Broom closets are generally 12-24in. wide and may incorporate one or two shelves and have one or two doors. Usually tall enough for brooms and mops and often used for storing vacuum cleaners and small kitchen steps.

**Watchpoint** Some have two doors that both have to be opened to take out large items.

## PANTRY UNITS

**Style** A tall cupboard used for storing food.

**In use** Some look like a broom closet – only the shelves are closer together. Others are pull-out pantry units that have wire racks attached to the door fascia so the whole interior slides out on runners.

**Watchpoint** They don't usually have any vents in them for fresh air to circulate, so should not be used for perishable food.

## APPLIANCE HOUSING UNITS

**Style** A tall cupboard for domestic appliances – typically single or double ovens.

**In use** Although you can get housing units for 'single' ovens to 'slide under' a counter, most people opt for a tall unit – 24in. wide – to take a single or double oven (and perhaps a microwave) so they are positioned further off the ground. Cupboards above and below the appliance provide space for pots and pans.

# WALL UNITS

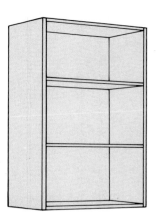

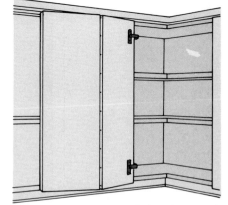

L-shaped corner unit

## STANDARD UNITS

**Style** The standard wall unit is a single or double cupboard 20in. or 40in. wide, with one or two shelves and doors (plain or glazed).

**In use** Wall cabinets are available in various heights ranging from 12-48 inches. The tallest can go right up to the ceiling. A variety of widths are also available and single unit doors can open either way.

## OPEN SHELVES

**Style** Plain shelves designed to be installed in a run of wall units. Rounded shelves for the end of a run of units are another option.

**In use** They are also available with gallery rails, which not only look decorative but are also handy to secure display plates and special tableware.

## CORNER UNITS

**Style** A wall unit that is designed to fit into a corner between two adjacent runs of units.

**In use** As with base corner units, two styles are available – straight and L-shaped.

**Watchpoint** Check which way the cupboard doors open and whether this is going to be convenient and safe in use.

# KITCHEN ACCESSORIES

## These additional accessories make a basic built-in kitchen more convenient.

Once your kitchen layout has been designed and the base, wall and tall cabinets chosen, there is a whole range of extras that can be built-in, on or under the basic units to make a kitchen easier or more efficient to use.

Most of these extras are additional compartments for storage of one sort or another; racks, drawers, bins, and so on. Others are hide-away features, such as ironing boards, tables, mixer support plinths or book rests.

Even matching cornices and valances are available to provide the finishing touches to your kitchen.

## EXTRAS FOR BASE UNITS

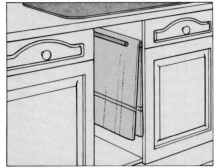

### TOWEL RAILS
**Style** Make use of odd spaces by fitting a telescopic towel rack to the underside of the counter over the space.
**In use** Ideally this should be positioned as close to the sink as possible.

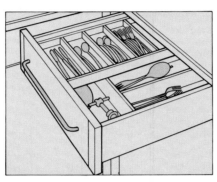

### CUTLERY TRAYS
**Style** All ranges of kitchen cabinets offer divided cutlery tray inserts to fit into drawers.
**In use** This helps you keep cutlery neat and tidy. Look for the double-decker inserts – these are two-tier, allowing you to store twice as much without everything becoming jumbled together.

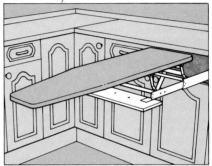

### IRONING BOARDS
**Style** A pull-out ironing board hidden behind a dummy drawer-front.
**In use** Not usually as large or as easy to use as a freestanding ironing board.

### GARBAGE BINS
**Style** In a built-in kitchen, there is often no space for a separate garbage bin. A bin positioned on the back of a cupboard door opens automatically when the door is opened. There is also one that fits into a deep drawer.
**In use** Takes up space within a cupboard.

### BASKETS
**Style** There are many types of wire baskets and racks that fit on the back of opening cupboard doors or into the cupboard itself.
**In use** Choose from those that hang like shelves, pull-out like drawers, or just stack.

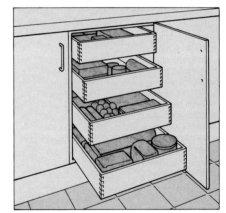

### PULL-OUTS
**Style** A door-fronted unit that has all-wood, old-fashioned drawers – called pull-outs – in it.
**In use** Can be more expensive than ordinary drawer units.

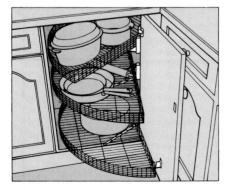

### CAROUSELS
**Style** A semi-circular, plastic-coated wire tray that fits on the inside of the opening door of a straight corner cupboard.
**In use** Generally more suited to storing things that are light in weight.

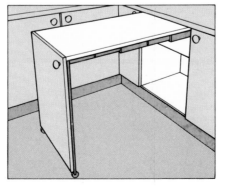

### PULL-OUT TABLES
**Style** There are various styles. This one fits behind a dummy door with casters. The whole unit pulls out on telescopic rails.
**In use** Provides a useful table or extra surface, pulls out to a maximum of the counter's width.

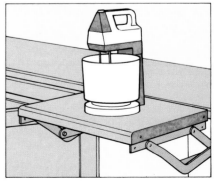

### MIXER SUPPORTS
**Style** Full-size mixers can be extremely heavy to get out of a cupboard.
**In use** A mixer support provides a solution – this is a spring-loaded table that swings up for use and away again into the base unit.

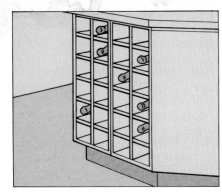

## WINE STORAGE

**Style** Wine racks are often available as alternatives to base units.

**In use** Typically, one rack fits into a 12in. space – two fit side-by-side in a unit. Bottles are stored on their sides.

## DECOR PANELS

**Style** Many appliances, such as dishwashers and refrigerators can be fitted with these fronts so that they blend in with rest of kitchen units.

**In use** They clip over the appliance's existing doors. Decor panels are only available for certain ranges of built-in kitchens.

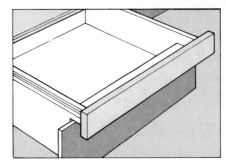

## TOE KICK DRAWERS

**Style** Special drawers that fit into the space under kitchen units.

**In use** Ideal for under-oven storage for baking tins and roasting trays.

Also look for a neat two-step ladder that fits into the toe kick space – excellent for reaching high wall cupboards.

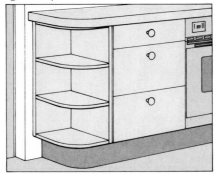

## OPEN SHELVES

**Style** A rounded open-shelving unit that fits at the end of a length of units.

**In use** These provide additional storage as well as being a neat way of finishing off the run.

## SMALLER DETAILS

When planning a kitchen, don't forget to consider future requirements for the services and the smaller accessories that add the finishing touches.

☐ Fit as many electrical outlets as possible – certainly no less than eight (four doubles) for an average-size kitchen – not including switched spur outlets for built-in appliances such as an electric range.

☐ Under-cupboard lights to illuminate work surfaces.

☐ Range hoods or exhaust fans.

☐ Dummy drawer fronts to conceal pull-out units such as ironing boards or foldaway tables or to disguise gaps between units.

☐ Molding to match your units.

☐ Extras for countertops such as inset sinks or cooktops, ceramic tile inserts for hot pans, or marble or Corian inserts as pastry slabs.

---

# OTHER ACCESSORIES

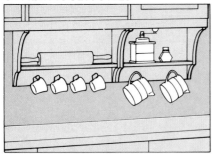

## MID-RANGE CUPBOARDS

**Style** Designed to fit in the wall space between base units and wall units.

**In use** Can be open shelves or have sliding doors – very useful for small jars, bottles and items that would get lost in a large cupboard.

## MID-RANGE CHOPPING BOARDS

**Style** A chopping board that folds away when not in use with a special rack behind for storing knives and cooking implements.

**In use** Handy – as these larger chopping boards are usually heavy and awkward to store.

## TALL UNIT FITTINGS

**Style** Some of the most useful extras you can buy for a tall unit are available, plastic-coated wire brackets or hooks for storing ironing boards, vacuum cleaners and accessories, saucepan lids, etc.

**In use** Most of these are readily available from sources other than the kitchen unit manufacturer, such as hardware and cookware shops.

---

# EXTRAS FOR WALL UNITS

## OPEN SHELVES

**Style** Rounded shelves that are wall-hung and finish off runs of wall units.

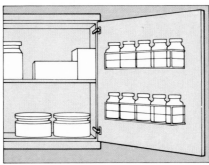

## SPICE RACKS

**Style** Assembled inside cupboard doors.

**In use** An easy-to-see way of storing small bottles and containers.

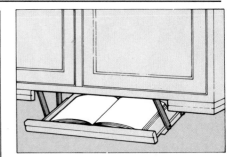

## BOOK REST

**Style** A drop-down book rest that, when closed, fits in with the molding below a wall unit.

**In use** Somewhere to place open cookbooks at eye-level – away from sticky work surfaces.

# RANGES, OVENS AND GRILLS

## Choose a range to suit the fuel you prefer, the size of your kitchen and the style of life you and your family lead.

Buying a range is not just a case of buying what fits, or looks best or costs the least. Fuel options and personal requirements are just a few of the points to consider before choosing an appliance that should last for many, many years.

The choice of fuel is probably your first consideration, followed by the style of range you would like to have. You can choose among conventional free-standing ranges; slide-in ranges; built-in/built-under ovens with a separate cooktop and a toaster oven or a microwave.

Think, too, about how much and what kind of cooking you do. A built-in half size oven and microwave with a separate cooktop may suit you better than a more conventional range with a full-size oven. The checkpoints below will help you decide.

### FUELS
**Electricity** is universally available and considered by many to be the fuel of the future with rarely any supply problems; but it can be expensive, hence the popularity of more economical appliances such as microwaves. Recent developments include halogen and magnetic induction heating methods.

**Gas** is a relatively inexpensive source of energy, usually more responsive than electricity. The majority of homes have a natural gas mains supply but homes in rural areas without gas mains have the liquid petroleum alternative, also known as lp gas. Piped in from bottles, cylinders or tanks stored outside, lp gas relies on regular deliveries for convenience.

Although many people like gas burners, gas ovens are a different story. Electric ovens maintain more even temperatures than gas units and their self-cleaning systems work better, too. Self-cleaning ovens in gas ranges, with a few exceptions, clean continuously. Electric ranges use a pyrolitic self-cleaning system that requires the oven to be turned to extremely high heat for a specified number of hours, reducing soil in the oven to fine ash. The cost of electricity may limit how often you use the self-cleaning feature.

### CHECKPOINTS
When choosing which type of range to buy bear in mind the following points:
☐ Changing from gas to electric or the other way around means installation expenses.
☐ Is your kitchen large enough for a separate oven and cooktop or would a conventional or slide-in stove save space?
When choosing an oven bear in mind:
☐ Shelves should be supported and not tip when partly pulled out.

☐ Glass doors enable food to be seen while cooking.
☐ Hinged doors should be reversible, able to be hung from either side.
☐ Drop down doors should be strong enough to support food and slope slightly towards the oven to prevent food slipping off.
☐ Removable doors and linings are easy to clean.
☐ Catalytic oven linings vaporize food splashes at medium to high temperatures making clean up simple.

☐ Pyrolytic oven linings remove food splashes completely at very high temperatures but are more expensive.
☐ An interior oven light helps judge cooking through glass doors without opening them.
☐ Make sure controls are easy to reach, easy to turn on and are clearly marked.
☐ If the broiler is inside the oven you won't be able to use them both at once.

## RANGES AND OVENS

### HIGH-LOW RANGE
**Style** A second oven, conventional or microwave, on top provides extra compact cooking capacity. Hob, oven and microwave are located in one central space. Ovens are available with self-cleaning feature. Range-hoods are optional.
**In use** Great for small kitchens as it compactly contains three cooking units in one. Available in gas or electric, with upper microwave or convection oven. Different types of cooktops are available as well.
**Watchpoints** A tall space is needed to fit. May not align perfectly with surrounding cabinets.

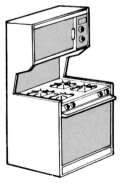

### SLIDE-IN RANGES
**Style** Sleek and uncluttered, they are designed to slide between kitchen units to create a flush look or even to fit across corners. Improved insulation allows them to touch adjacent units and be installed next to refrigerators.
**In use** They can be gas or electric and some slide-ins now have dual fuel options, with gas cooktop and electric fan oven being the most popular combination, although halogen cooktops are available on some. The broiler can be separate at waist height or in the oven.
**Watchpoints** Look for adjustable feet to align with adjacent units.

## BUILT-IN/BUILT-UNDER OVENS

**Style** Also known as split level ranges as the cooktops are installed separately. They have a streamlined appearance and can be a single oven with or without integral grill, double oven or oven and microwave. The latest innovations usually appear on built-in appliances first.

**In use** Can be installed at a height or in a position that suits you best, making it ideal for people with back problems or to keep the oven out of reach of children. Allows you to have a combination of fuels – a gas cooktop and electric oven – and also to choose between different manufacturers.

**Watchpoints** Cost is the main disadvantage as they require a supporting housing unit.

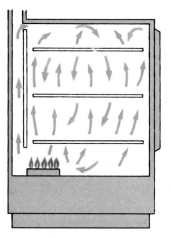

## FREESTANDING RANGE

**Style** Traditionally, these consist of a single oven, combined with a cooktop and a broiler that can either be in a drawer below the oven or inside the oven itself.

**In use** They are either gas or electric. Electric ranges require a 30 or more amp box and a heavy-duty cable. Gas ranges are connected to the gas supply using a flexible hose that can be turned off and disconnected. Models with two roller feet can be moved easily; the other two feet should be adjustable to enable the range to be sited perfectly level.

**Watchpoints** Freestanding ranges are the most difficult to fit neatly into a run of built-in units. Check whether the insulation is good enough to place next to a refrigerator or food cupboard.

## COOKING METHODS

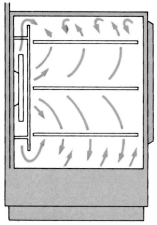

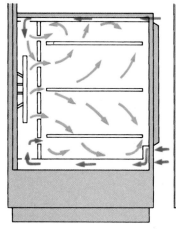

### NATURAL CONVECTION

Has a slightly drying effect when cooking – an advantage for some foods. For traditional cooks and those who do not need to batch bake.

### FAN-ASSISTED/DUCTED FORCED CONVECTION

Use various methods to keep temperatures even throughout the oven. Fan-assisted ovens (above) circulate air around the oven, ducted fans (right) send heated air through ducts at shelf levels. Does not require pre-heating therefore economical, especially if you can fill each shelf, and lower cooking temperatures mean fewer splashes. Food keeps moist and shrinks less. Some of the most sophisticated models have a temperature probe for accurate roasting. The hum or vibration from the fan can be annoying. Mostly found on electric ovens but sometimes available on gas models.

### MULTI-FUNCTION OVENS

Has a wide range of functions – natural convection, fan-assisted, bottom heat only, top heat only, defrost and automatic roast (sealing at a high temperature before temperature automatically lowers) are the most commonly available. Most frequently found on electric built-in ovens.

## BROILERS

The position of the broiler depends on the type of range – eye-level broilers are only available on conventional ranges or inside a built-in oven. Otherwise the broiler is located below the oven, in a pull-out drawer or inside the oven itself. A broiler set inside the oven means you cannot broil and bake at the same time – if this is likely to be a problem, consider buying a table-top broiler. Make sure the broiler pan handles are secure and that it is large enough for your needs. A reversible broiler rack and two shelf positions make a separate broiler more versatile.

### GAS

Gas broilers either have a series of jets along the back or along two sides, or the flames work out from a central plate. Gas broilers can be adjusted by lowering the jets.

### ELECTRIC

Electric broilers have a single or double element – the former for small portions. Rotisserie and kebab attachments are available for some broilers but do not buy them unless you are sure you will make full use of them.

gas grill

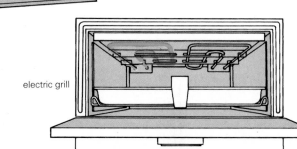

electric grill

# COOKTOPS, MICROWAVES AND TOASTER OVENS

Hobs can be gas, electric or dual fuel, sold separately or as part of a range.

## HOBS

Either gas or electric, part of a conventional range or separately built-in. Most built-in hobs are for the right-handed; if you are left-handed, look for reversible controls.

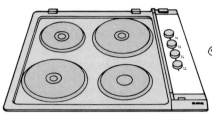

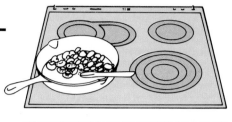

### ELECTRIC RADIANT BURNERS

**Style** Usually found on freestanding ranges and a few built-in hobs.

**In use** Modern rings respond faster than earlier models. Look for dual circuit rings where the inner ring only can be switched on for economy when using small pans.

**Watchpoints** Built-in radiant hobs are deep so you may lose drawer space underneath. Tops may be awkward to clean even though they hinge or the spill tray slides out.

### ELECTRIC SEALED/SOLID

**Style** The electric element is covered by a thin metal sheet.

**In use** Easier to clean and less space consuming than radiant versions. Look for a range of hot plate sizes and low settings or pan savers that keep foods at a steady simmer or prevent liquids from boiling over. May also be available as large rectangular shapes for fish kettles.

**Watchpoints** Not as responsive as radiant rings.

### ELECTRIC CERAMIC

**Style** Attractive streamlined appearance and can double as an extra worktop when cool (but do not use as a cutting surface).

**In use** Some ceramic hobs have dual circuit control for economy when using small pans.

**Watchpoints** Should have residual heat indicators as a safety feature. You may need a new set of pans for maximum contact on the very flat surface. Standard ceramic hobs not as fast as radiant or sealed ones.

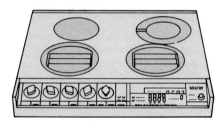

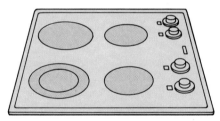

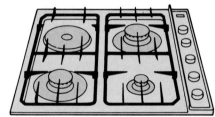

### HALOGEN CERAMIC

**Style** A recent invention. Some models have four cooking zones, others five and some may combine two halogen zones with two conventional electric ceramic areas.

**In use** The tungsten halogen filament produces an instant heat when turned on and the range of temperatures can be controlled very precisely. The cooking area glows red when on.

**Watchpoints** Not widely available and expensive at the present time.

### MAGNETIC INDUCTION CERAMIC

**Style** The electric hob of the future, it uses a magnetic coil under a ceramic surface.

**In use** The coil generates magnetic energy only when a ferrous pan is in place; the pan and its contents get hot while the hob surface remains cool.

**Watchpoints** Not widely available and very expensive at the present. You may have to replace your existing cooking pans.

### DUAL FUEL

**Style** Usually two gas burners and two sealed electric rings on the same hob. May also come as three-gas/one-electric combination.

**In use** Ideal if you want to combine the features of both fuels.

**Watchpoint** They usually cost more than the single-fuel equivalent.

### GAS BURNERS

**Style** The gas burners are set in a recessed tray covered by stainless steel or enameled pan supports. The supports usually lift off in two or four parts for cleaning. All four burners may be the same size or there may be two large and two small, the latter for cooking at a low heat. Most modern stoves have spark ignition, which is electrical, to light the burners.

**In use** The gas burners can be adjusted simply and quickly. Some hobs have thermostatically controlled burners that adjust the flame to maintain a previously set heat.

**Watchpoint** Look for a slim divider between controls and burners on built-in hobs to protect controls from excessive heat. An automatic re-ignition device, which relights a burner that has gone out, is a useful safety feature. Check that the pan supports are able to carry very small pans.

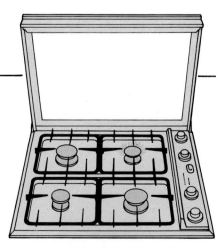

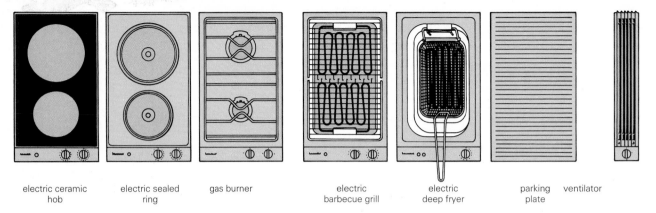

electric ceramic hob    electric sealed ring    gas burner    electric barbecue grill    electric deep fryer    parking plate    ventilator

## MODULAR GAS OR ELECTRIC

**Style** These are half-width hobs that can be installed in any combination. The choice includes electric ceramic, sealed ring, grill and deep-fat fryer and gas burners. A parking plate to rest pans is a useful addition.

**In use** Ideal for a very small kitchen or for the cook who has very specific needs. A surface-mounted ventilator grill is also available.

**Watchpoint** More expensive than conventional hobs.

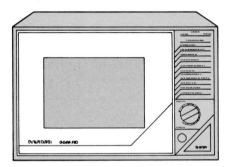

△ The basic microwave has manual settings with or without a rotating turntable.

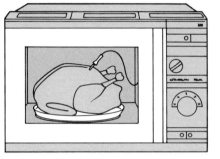

△ A rotating antenna in floor or ceiling and temperature probe adds versatility.

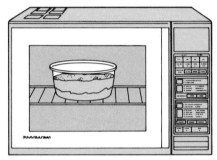

△ Electronic settings and an internal shelf featured on some expensive models.

## MICROWAVE OVENS

Microwaves can be used to defrost, cook and reheat food. Capacity is limited, so unless cooking for one or two they must be used in conjunction with conventional oven and hob.

They work using a magnetron that produces waves that vibrate the water molecules in the food; this causes friction and heat that does the cooking. The process is fast and the oven needs no warm-up period so it is energy saving and economical. The short cooking time means that vitamins and minerals are retained in the food.

Porcelain, ceramic, glass, plastic, cardboard and paper containers can be used safely and clean up is reduced as food can be cooked and served in the same dish. Never use metal or foil containers or china that has a gold or silver trim as this damages the magnetron.

Most ovens are countertop models; some can be wall-mounted or built-in.

**Controls** The simplest and cheapest ovens have a manual timer setting up to about 30 minutes with two power levels – a low one for defrosting and slow cooking and a high one for reheating and fast cooking. More expensive and sophisticated models have electronic controls with timers that can be set up to 2 hours, programming facilities that enable pre-setting of a series of operations such as defrost, followed by cooking and finally keeping warm. These models also have a choice of power levels.

A temperature probe attached inside the oven and inserted into the center of the food can be set to a particular temperature and gives a far more accurate method of cooking. When the food reaches the set heat the oven switches to keeping the food warm.

**Interior layout** Food must be turned at least once in the oven during the process to ensure even cooking. This is done by hand on the cheapest models; medium priced models have a rotating turntable that turns during cooking but this can restrict the space in an oven or the shape of dish you can use. More expensive ovens have a rotating antenna beneath or above the floor or ceiling that gives an even distribution of microwaves. They may also have a shelf that is useful for stacking several shallow dishes in the oven at one time.

**Combination oven** A microwave oven on its own cannot boil eggs, deep fry, cook pastry or apple pie. It is not successful for large roasts or a large number of baked potatoes, and food can look pale and bland even when cooked. To overcome this, ovens that combine microwave, broiling and convection methods of cooking have been developed. This means a choice between a microwave, broiling or convection cooking or any combination of microwave/convection broiler.

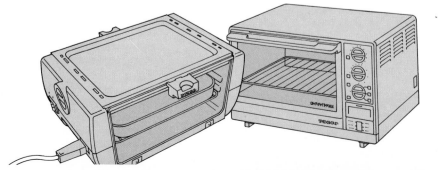

## TOASTER OVENS

There are many small electric ovens available. They do not replace a conventional oven but are a useful addition. Most cook using the convection method with an internal broiler for browning or broiling. Some have a steaming facility, which is particularly good for fish or vegetables.

# REFRIGERATORS AND FREEZERS

## Choose the most convenient and economical refrigerator or freezer to meet your needs.

### REFRIGERATORS

The size and style of refrigerator and freezer you choose depend on the size of your household and your pocketbook. However, your cooking and shopping habits must be accounted for as well.

**Size** To estimate the capacity your family needs, allow 12 cubic feet of total refrigerator and freezer space for the first two adults in your household, then add 2 more cubic feet for each additional member. A family of four, then, will buy a refrigerator-freezer with a capacity of 16 cubic feet.

As you make a selection, be aware that the fuller a refrigerator or freezer is kept, the less it costs to run. Especially where electricity costs are high, this offers a compelling reason not to buy a refrigerator or freezer too large for your household or for the amount of food you normally keep on hand.

**Door configurations** Top freezer, bottom freezer, side-by-side — which arrangement of compartments makes most sense for your family?

**Single-door refrigerators** have only a small freezer compartment on top. These are inexpensive to buy, but the freezer temperature usually is not low enough for long-term storage.

**Two-door refrigerators** have separate freezers at the top or bottom. These will maintain food for long periods of time. Bottom-freezer models put everyday items such as milk, eggs, and soft drinks at eye level. Pull-out baskets facilitate access to frozen foods down below.

**Side-by-side units** have two and sometimes three doors, providing eye-level storage in both refrigerator and freezer. Side-by-side models are wider than up-and-down versions, and their narrow shelves cannot handle bulky items such as a large frozen turkey.

**Watchpoints** Keep in mind good design features when you shop for a refrigerator or freezer. Smooth, seamless interiors are easier to keep clean than those interrupted by seams or obstructions. Glass shelves are much easier to wash than wire grids, but they are more fragile. If the shelves on the interior of the door are removable, they will be much simpler to clean.

Controls near the front are accessible without removing bottles or other containers. Make sure the refrigerator you buy can hold tall bottles for upright storage. Door shelves should have room for taller jars and bottles too. Make certain some of the interior shelves are adjustable. Ice-makers in the freezer may become a maintenance problem; they add to energy costs.

More manufacturers now offer 24in. deep models that do not stick out beyond the front edges of counters. Built-in or freestanding, 24in. deep designs help minimize the bulk of this massive piece of kitchen equipment. Shallower refrigerators and freezers are wider than standard models, however, and often are taller as well, so allocate kitchen space accordingly.

**Leaving room** All refrigerators and freezers require adequate air circulation, so when sliding a refrigerator into a run of kitchen units, make sure that you leave about 4in. of space above and at the back. Most built-ins provide grille work for ventilation, so you don't have to leave space around these models.

### FEATURES CHECKLIST
**Before buying a refrigerator consider which features you require:**
- ☐ Salad bin/drawers
- ☐ Dairy shelf
- ☐ Frozen food compartment
- ☐ Interior light
- ☐ Drinks dispenser
- ☐ Ice maker
- ☐ Adjustable feet (to alter height of refrigerator)
- ☐ Egg storage
- ☐ Automatic defrost
- ☐ Shelf for standing bottles
- ☐ Warning lights

## TYPES OF REFRIGERATORS

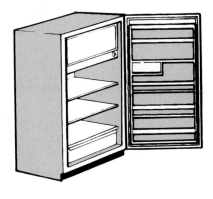

**SINGLE DOOR**
This model usually has a manual defrost and limited freezer capacity.

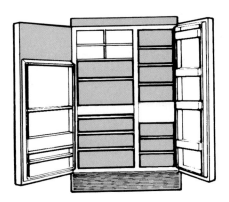

**SIDE-BY-SIDE**
Offering the greatest access to both compartments, it requires the least door-swing clearance in front.

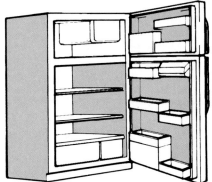

**TOP FREEZER**
The freezer and refrigerator sections are separate, usually with automatic defrosting.

## FREEZERS

Preserving food by freezing is relatively quick, simple and effective. Freeze homemade food, fresh food or simply store frozen goods so that you are prepared for unexpected visitors, unplanned meals or meals that you can knock out in a minute.

**Safe temperature** The food is packed and frozen at a temperature of 0° – 10° or even below. This provides a safe

environment where bacteria cannot multiply. The storage period varies depending on the particular food, but commercially frozen food can be stored for up to three months and your own fresh/home-cooked food for much longer.

**Size** Size and dimensions are up to you and your needs, but freezers generally range from the tabletop size to countertop-height upright models (10 cubic feet), taller uprights (up to 20 cubic feet) to the largest chest freezer (25 cubic feet).

**Features** For those who pre-freeze food in their freezer (rather than loading it with pre-frozen foods), a fast-freeze facility on a freezer overrides the thermostat to ensure that the temperature is sufficiently low to freeze fresh food without affecting the load already frozen.

For a list of the types of features available on modern freezers see our checklist.

## DEFROSTING

**Fridges** Some need to be defrosted manually by disconnecting the power and allowing the frost that forms in the refrigerator, to thaw. Others defrost automatically – they are referred to as frost-free and defrost on a day-to-day basis, so there is never any build-up of frost. Semi-automatic defrosting types are press-button operated.

**Freezers** Although you can buy frost-free freezers too, many still defrost manually. But life is made easier for the freezer owner by a draining spout at the base of a freezer. When the freezer has defrosted, the water runs out through the spout so all that is required is a bucket under the spout to catch the water. In other models water collects in a removable tray in the base.

## FREEZER FEATURES CHECKLIST

- ☐ Adjustable feet
- ☐ Lock
- ☐ Interior light
- ☐ Automatic defrost
- ☐ Defrost spout
- ☐ Baskets
- ☐ Separate drawer compartments
- ☐ Freezer drawer for soft fruits
- ☐ Fast freeze facility

## TYPES OF FREEZER

### CHEST

**Style** This has a top-opening lid. Originally a chest freezer was a long rectangular shape but squat, box-shaped freezers with top-opening lids are now available. Sizes range in capacity from about 10 cubic ft. up to 25 cubic ft.

**In use** Frozen food is usually organized inside the chest in removable wire baskets or trays, which makes packing and retrieving food easier than simply piling it in.

**Watchpoint** The nature of the rectangular-shaped chest freezer means that it takes up a relatively large area of floor space in your kitchen and many chest freezers are kept in a utility room or even the garage. Most models are lockable to make them secure.

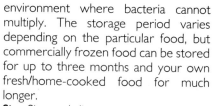

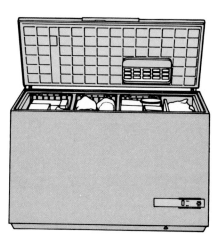

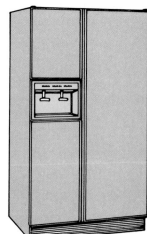

### UPRIGHT

**Style** This has a front-opening door and comes in a variety of heights ranging from tabletop size to countertop-height and above.

**In use** Takes up less floor space than the chest freezer and also can be integrated into a built-in kitchen, as most are available with frames to which cupboard door fascias can be attached to match kitchen units. Food is usually organized in pull-out drawers or baskets.

### ICE CUBER

**Style** This 34 ½in. ice maker makes up to 51 lbs. of ice in 24 hours. It filters out minerals to let the flavor of your beverage come through. It is available in a variety of finish colors.

**In use** Unit shuts off automatically when storage bin is full. Requires 1 ¼in. drain and water tubing kit.

### REFRIGERATOR-FREEZER

**Style** Big models usually have two opening doors (they are like two upright models next to each other) and apart from being much larger than standard models, are more expensive.

**In use** These often contain ice-making machines and cold drink dispensers. Ice or drink, is dispensed through an opening on the outside of the door, which means you don't have to open the door every time you want to use this facility.

# KITCHEN SINKS

Bright and cheerful, today's sinks come in a host of materials and colors with a choice of practical accessories.

## MATERIALS

**Stainless steel** is still the most popular choice for a kitchen sink. It's tough, hardwearing, lightweight and well-priced with many designs at the budget-end of the price range. It can be pressed into almost any space and easily hole-punched to take a range of faucets and accessories. A drawback with stainless steel sinks is the clatter of china and cutlery on it, so make sure you choose a sink with a vibration damper underneath – just look for a black pad stuck to the underneath of the sink. Your sink should also be grounded to prevent the risk of getting an electric shock. Although you can do this yourself, it is advisable to contact a qualified electrician to do the work for you.

**Vitreous enamel** can have a matt or a gloss finish, which is baked onto cast iron, or more often these days onto pressed steel. These sinks used to have a bad reputation for chipping easily, but manufacturers are successfully overcoming this problem by applying a much thinner coat of enamel to make it more chip-resistant. The edges of the sink are still the most vulnerable point, though, so treat them with care. Enameled sinks are heat- and stain-resistant, but you should clean them with a non-abrasive liquid or cream household cleaner to avoid scratches.

**Ceramic** or fireclay sinks are available in modern shapes, sizes and colors. New ones are scratchproof and almost non-chip; they're virtually stain-resistant too.

(These properties are all improvements on the older types, which were prone to scratching, crazing and chipping.)

**Brass** has a tendency to scratch and it must be cleaned with a proper brass cleaner followed by a regular polish with a brass product. Available as a sink/drainer unit or separate components, including faucets.

**Corian** is a cast, man-made stone that looks and feels like marble, though it is far tougher, stain- and heat-resistant. The sinks come in different sizes and can be permanently bonded to a matching continuous work surface. Any tiny scratches can easily be erased with an abrasive cleaner or very fine sandpaper. Corian is very expensive but virtually indestructible.

**Asterite** is a tough blend of silica and resin, with the color running right through the material. It has a very high resistance to heat, stains and scratches and is also easy to clean.

**Polycarbonate** is another man-made material that is available in a number of manufacturers' lines. It can cope with temperatures up to 302°F and has some noise-absorbing qualities as well.

**Fradura** is a molded rock-like composite material made up from glass and minerals, chemically bonded with resin. Impact and stain-resistant, it withstands temperatures up to 392°F.

## SIZES

Inset sinks sit in a hole cut in the work surface and offer the widest choice of shapes and sizes. Consider what size you want the sink to be. Choose from single sink and drainer, double sink and drainer, or sink and double drainer.

Where space is limited, a combination of one-and-a-half sinks plus a drainer offers practical use of space. A half-bowl usually measures about half (or even a quarter) of the size of a standard sink – ideal for fitting a waste disposer. Always go for the largest possible sink to fit the available space.

What looks like an extremely shallow bowl (1-3in. deep) is best employed as a drainer – although it comes in handy for washing or straining vegetables, as it has its own drain.

When space is really tight, separate sinks and drainers are the most versatile as you can put them as close or as far apart as you like.

You could, of course, go without a drainer. Many modern sinks come with draining racks that fit into them to hold clean dishes, pots and pans. (See 'Optional extras' next page).

**Bowl sizes** vary enormously from the smallest round sinks – 15in. in diameter – to a big, rectangular bowl 18in. wide. Most sinks should measure at least 6-7in. deep for practical reasons.

Check that the largest item you need to wash on a regular basis fits into it. Some sinks come with pre-made holes for taps and accessories, others give you the option to have the holes punched out where you require them. (Most faucet holes are about 1½in. in diameter.)

Standard wastes are 1½in. in diameter or a larger 3½in. for a strainer waste – this incorporates a removable strainer that catches scraps of food etc. Decide at this stage whether you want a waste disposer – most fit the 3½in. drain, which is the most practical size.

All sinks are made to fit countertops that are between 1-2in. thick.

## STYLES OF SINK

### SELF-RIMMED
**Style** Made of stainless steel, enamel or ceramic, it comes in various colors and styles.
**In use** Self-rimming sinks not only look good, but often can be fitted over edges of existing sink openings so that no additional counter cutting is required. They are easy to clean.

### STEEL-RIMMED
**Style** A steel rim fits around this type of sink, is also available in a variety of colors and styles.
**In use** The steel gives a neat look and hides any ragged laminate edges around the opening. Rim joint can be hard to keep clean.

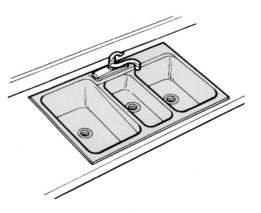

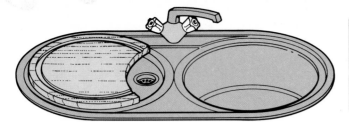

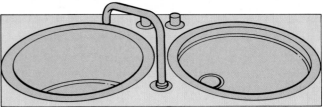

## INSET CIRCULAR
**Style** A variation on the rectangular shape.
**In use** The deep sink is for washing up, the shallow sink is ideal for washing vegetables but is intended as a drainer. It could be fitted with a waste disposer unit so peelings and the like can be pushed straight down the drain. A wooden cover/chopping board for the drainer is often an optional extra.

## SEPARATE CIRCULAR UNITS
**Style** Separate sink and drainer – fit snugly into corners of countertops.
**In use** Particularly good where space is limited as they are available in small sizes (18in. in diameter – although there are bigger ones available). Choose from stainless steel or enameled steel versions. A draining basket is available to set in the bowl and a teak chopping board/cover fits neatly over the drainer.

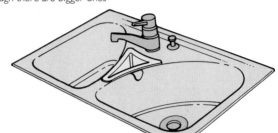

## SEPARATE SQUARE UNITS
**Style** Inset square bowl and drainer made as separate units.
**In use** These are designed to give maximum flexibility, so if necessary they can be inset into countertops at opposite ends of your kitchen. Each unit measures about 20 × 20in. The drainer is available with a half-sink incorporated. These are made in stainless steel, enameled steel and most other materials, including ceramic.

## TRIANGULAR
**Style** Triangular-shaped sink and drainer set into a rectangular normal-sized sink unit. Also available with a compact half-bowl, built in.
**In use** Sink and drainer set at an angle to each other. This looks attractive and many people also find the positioning of the sink very comfortable to use. Available in stainless steel, enameled steel, or man-made plastic-related materials.

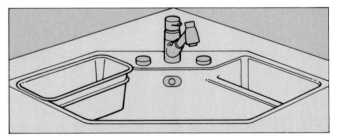

## DROP-IN LAUNDRY
**Style** One-piece, self-rimmed fiberglass molding is leak and stain resistant. Includes rubber stopper, raised soap dish and drain assembly.
**In use** Perfect for washing clothing or for other large cleanups. Usually found in basement or utility room. Installs in standard cutout countertop.

## CORNER
**Style** A sink that cuts corners! Designed to fit into corners that might normally be wasted space.
**In use** This inset sink sits diagonally across a corner area. The large sink is for washing-up, the other two for rinsing and drying. Available in a variety of materials.
**Watchpoint** Mixer faucet should swivel and also be long enough to reach over the smaller bowls.

---

## OPTIONAL EXTRAS

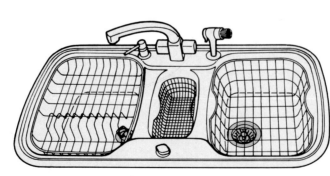

## PERFORATED DRAINER
Made of plastic, this thick perforated tray fits over the sink. Useful for draining and straining. Although the flat variety (shown) is most useful, some manufacturers offer perforated bowls that sit in the sink itself.

## DRAINER
Plastic-coated wire basket – often incorporating a plate drainer – sits over the top of a bowl so that once the dishes have been washed they can drain over it. This is ideal for those who only have a sink and no drainer.

## BASKET
This is also made from plastic-coated wire. It sits inside the main bowl to protect your crockery from chipping or cracking while washing up.

## CHOPPING BOARD/COVER
Wooden cover (usually made from teakwood) to put over the main sink when not in use. It doubles up as a chopping board, so is ideal in small kitchens. When the sink is not being used, you can use it as a food preparation surface.

# CHOOSING KITCHEN FAUCETS

## Today's faucets are no longer just a way to turn the water on and off, but a stylish addition to any kitchen.

## MATERIALS

The look and the feel of your kitchen faucets is mainly governed by the material they are made from.

**Brass** This is the base metal for most faucets. However, solid brass or brass-plated faucets are the perfect accent for period-style kitchen units. They can be polished with a high shine or be given an antiqued finish.

**Chrome** Generally the cheapest type of material from which faucets are made. Chromium plate suits all styles of sinks and kitchens and is usually offered on nearly all faucet designs.

**Porcelain** Not used for modern faucets, although porcelain decoration on period-style faucets is experiencing something of a revival at the present — mostly teamed up with brass.

**Nylon** Highly colored nylon faucets are a good way to brighten up a plain sink or kitchen. Very hardwearing, they stay cool even when you're running the hot water through them. They're easy to clean too.

**Enamel** Some of the brightest colored faucets have an enamel finish, baked on to a metal base to give a tough finish.

## HOW FAUCETS WORK

In a conventional type of faucet the valve and washer are the parts that operate the flow of water. But on the most modern type of faucet the valve and washer are replaced by a ceramic disc or cartridge. These are claimed to work more efficiently as the disc is supposed to be virtually immune to wear and tear or corrosion from water and lime build-up. This should reduce the chance of leaks and drips and should therefore last longer.

**Valves and washers** are still found on many faucets that you buy today, though; the newest types are coated with a non-stick finish to prevent hard-water deposits from forming on them.

## MAKING A CHOICE

The decision to purchase a particular faucet should be based on ease of operation, durability of both the finish and the operating mechanism and the ease of cleaning. Test out the unit before you buy it, making sure you are comfortable with the way it works. Grip the handle, raise and lower the temperature, be sure the spout moves with ease, operate the sprayer or any extras it may be equipped with. In general, the larger the movement of the handle, the easier it is to adjust the temperature and flow.

Those with young children or arthritic family members may wish to steer clear from round faucet knobs and individual levers since these require finger pressure for operation. Instead, choose a single-lever model, which is easier to operate.

Be sure to purchase a faucet with a swivel spout; stationary spouts are really only suitable for a bathroom. Also, if you have a sink that has more than one bowl, make sure that the spout is long or high enough for you to direct water into both bowls.

The finish on faucets must be able to withstand corrosion and wear. Gold-toned fixtures in particular have a problem with chipping and peeling. Also, finely decorated handles are hard to keep clean. Opt for a material with great durability such as chrome or brass.

Decide on the sort of faucets you want before buying a sink, then you can make sure you order one with the correct faucet holes. Choose faucets that will fit in with the rest of your kitchen's style. Also, look for manufacturers who make coordinating sinks and faucets in matching colors and finishes.

**Styles** There are four basic choices in faucet design: ball-type, cartridge, disc and compression. Many faucets look the same outwardly but are constructed differently on the inside. Be sure you know what you are getting before you make your selection.

Most washerless types of faucets, (ball-type, cartridge and disc) are controlled with a single handle. However, there are some that use two handles. This type of faucet has less trouble than the average compression faucet and is designed for quick repair.

Many double-handled faucets are compression designed. Unlike the other faucets, they contain washers or seals that must be replaced occasionally. Replacements are easily made and the parts are inexpensive.

## FAUCET TYPES

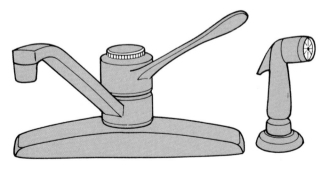

### SINGLE HANDLE FAUCET
The majority of washerless faucets are controlled with a single handle. There are three types: ball-type, cartridge and disc.

### DOUBLE HANDLE FAUCET
Most double handle faucets are compression designed. They contain washers and seals that must be replaced.

## MIXER FAUCETS

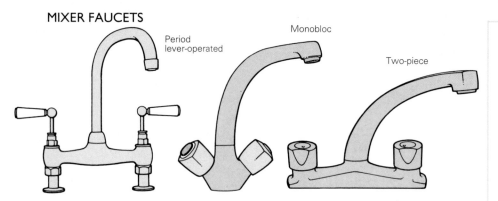

Period lever-operated

Monobloc

Two-piece

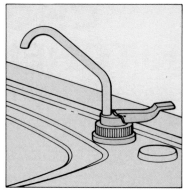

### CONVENTIONAL
**Style** These faucets are conventional in the sense that they have the 'conventional' workings – they all operate with a valve and washer. However, they vary widely in style from a brass, period-type, lever-operated mixer (which is two-piece so requires two tapholes) to the more modern-looking monobloc and two-piece mixers made from brightly colored enamel and shiny chromium plate with encased heads.
**In use** They all obviously combine hot and cold water in one spout – and have swivel spouts.

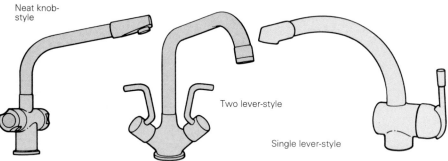

Neat knob-style

Two lever-style

Single lever-style

### QUARTER-TURN
**Style** Monobloc mixers all fitted with ceramic discs – water comes on/off by a quarter turn.
**In use** Choose from a mixer with neat knobs (can be tricky to turn with greasy/wet hands), or a single lever that turns one way for hot and the other for cold water (lever can go either side of spout to suit right- or left-handers), or the mixer with long levers that can be operated by elbows.

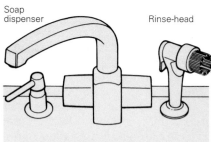

Soap dispenser

Rinse-head

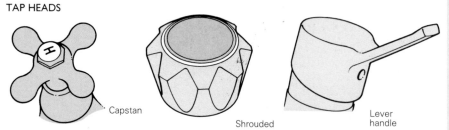

Spatula attachment

### ACCESSORIES
A **'rinse head'** is a brush connected to a flexible hose (hidden under the counter) which lifts out for use. When a lever is pressed it sends a spray of water onto the dirty dishes. This is handy if you have a sink that incorporates a bowl with a wire basket in it – once the dishes are washed they can be 'hosed down' while sitting in the basket. You can buy interchangeable heads for it such as a **spatula** to scrape pots and pans.
A **soap dispenser** holds liquid soap (dishwashing liquid) under the sink in a reservoir. When the small 'faucet' on top of the sink is pressed, it squirts soap into the sink.

### TAP HEADS

Capstan

Shrouded

Lever handle

There are three basic types of handle: the traditional **capstan head** with the cross top often called a cross head, the modern **shrouded or encased head** made of plastic or metal or the **lever handle**.
The capstan head – the traditional design – has a center screw that secures the head onto the rest of the faucet. The shrouded head is a distinctive chunky style – the fixing screw is hidden under a cap on the top of the head. The lever handle faucet has a lever to operate the faucet. The same color and material as the body of the tap, it works when it is pressed up/down or from side to side.

### HOT WATER DISPENSERS
This is a faucet with a difference. It is mounted on your sink top alongside your ordinary hot and cold taps and provides instant steaming hot water. A press of the lever draws up boiling water from a tank stored beneath the sink. It is a quick and economical alternative to boiling an electric kettle as it can be used to make tea, coffee, gravy, stocks, etc, and costs less to operate than a 40-watt bulb.
**Watchpoint** The water really is boiling – so young children shouldn't have access to it.

### CHECKLIST
☐ Do the faucets and sink unit look right together?
☐ Are there enough tapholes in the sink to accommodate the faucets you have chosen?
☐ Consider the height of faucets if sink is used to fill buckets etc.
☐ Choose faucets that fit in with the overall look of the kitchen – plastic faucets might not suit a traditional-style room.
☐ Faucets must be hardwearing. Porcelain faucets in the kitchen might not be as suitable as in the bathroom.
☐ If any type of hose – for the garden or for a washing machine – has to be fitted to the faucets, make sure the faucets are suitable.
☐ Think of cleaning – don't choose faucets that require a lot of work.
☐ If faucets are for someone elderly, ensure they can use them.
☐ Some of the chunkier faucet heads might look attractive, but try them out in the shop to see if they are easily turned on – even if your hands are wet or sticky.

# GARBAGE DISPOSERS AND BINS

## Clean and efficient ways of getting rid of kitchen waste.

The frightening thing about kitchen waste is the sheer volume that is created in the average home. A lot of this is due to modern packaging materials – particularly cardboard wrapping, plastic containers and metal cans – but a good part of your garbage is likely to be leftover food, vegetable waste, or fish and meat bones, which tend to smell, attract flies and generally be a nuisance.

At one time, of course, garbage disposal could be kept to a minimum: vegetable waste went on the compost heap, spare food was fed to the animals, anything combustible went into the stove and only metal things really needed to be thrown away. But these days things are different – not all households have a compost heap, so decaying matter has to be disposed of hygienically and all other garbage put out for the garbage collector.

**A recycling center** With today's environmental concerns, a recycling bin has become a must in the kitchen. The most useful unit is one that fits neatly into a cabinet and consists of three or more separated bins. A recycling center should provide sections for glass, paper, plastic and aluminum. In many areas recycling has become mandatory. Many manufacturers have created systems that make recycling an attractive option.

**A waste disposer** fitted to the kitchen sink is an ideal way of getting rid of food scraps and waste. Usually electrically operated, it fits underneath the sink and converts food waste into a fine slurry, which is washed away down into the drains. There are two main types of electric waste disposer – batch-feed or continuous feed. With the batch feed type, you load up the waste disposer, put the cover/lid on and turn it to start it up. The continuous-feed type has a separate switch that you turn on to activate the disposer – waste material is then fed into it. (If you have children it is more advisable to go for the batch-feed disposer as this only works when the lid is in place.) With both types, cold water is left running into the sink during operation to facilitate the process.

With all types of disposers it is advisable to get approval from your local authority before it is installed.

Most waste disposers are designed to fit the larger (3½in.) size of drain outlet (fitted to some sinks with a basket strainer).

Waste disposers can get jammed if fed with non-disposable waste. Some disposers have automatic reversing which will unjam obstructions, others have a manually operated reversing switch or a release key (like a small wrench) for clearing jams.

A disposer needs its own 1½in. waste pipe, fitted with a P-trap or an S-trap, leading to the main soil stack. Some have an additional connection to which a dishwasher drain hose can be attached which cuts down the number of waste pipes passing through the wall.

**Bins** In addition to a waste disposer you will also need a garbage bin. This can either be freestanding or positioned inside a kitchen cupboard, either within the drawers or on the back of a door. Waste bins come in different materials (mainly plastic or metal) that are easy to keep clean, particularly if the bin can be fitted with an inner bin or a bin liner.

**Compactor** Where a lot of household waste is created, a compactor is useful. You simply feed garbage into a large removable container inside a pull-down or pull-out drawer. When the unit is switched on, the garbage is compressed to around a quarter of its volume. At the same time the compressed garbage is packed into neat sacks, which makes disposal easier. A domestic compactor will usually fit neatly into a cabinet or under a work surface.

## GARBAGE DISPOSERS

### CONTINUOUS-FEED DISPOSER
**Style** An unobtrusive electrically powered device that fits beneath the kitchen sink.
**In use** The switch for a continuous-feed waste disposer is usually mounted on the wall or on the front of kitchen cupboards and once turned on, vegetable and food waste can be fed into the machine with the cold tap left running. Some models have a reversing switch to free light jams (some others are automatically reversing), to free major jams a small wrench or release key is usually supplied.
**Watchpoint** A perforated disc prevents cutlery from accidentally falling into the machine when not in use and a rubber 'baffle' prevents water and waste from splashing out during use.

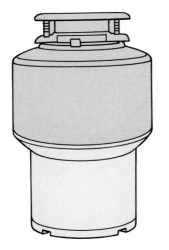

### BATCH-FEED DISPOSER
**Style** Very similar in appearance to a continuous-feed machine, the batch-feed disposer fits under the kitchen sink too.
**In use** The on/off switch for this type of waste disposer is usually incorporated in the inlet neck. After a batch of waste has been put into the machine, the neck is rotated to turn the disposer on and rotated again to turn it off. A second load can then be added.
**Watchpoint** Generally more expensive than continuous-feed models, but because it only works with lid on, its major plus point is the safety aspect – important for those with young children.

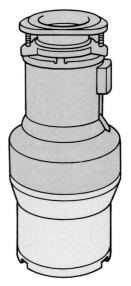

## TRASH COMPACTORS

**Style** An electrically operated machine that fits in place of a kitchen cupboard and can be fitted with a matching decor panel. It is usually about half the width of a dishwasher.

**In use** The pull-out drawer of the compactor is fitted with its own plastic or water-resistant paper bags. After the garbage has been put in, the machine applies a compressing force of about a ton, which reduces the volume of the garbage by 75 percent.

**Watchpoint** To prevent young children operating the machine, a removable safety key is provided.

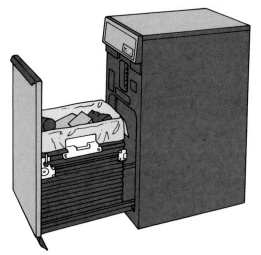

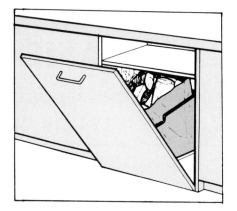

## RECYCLING BIN

In recent years, the recycling bin has become a household necessity. With the great concern for the environment, recycling is now mandatory in many areas across the country. This means there must be a place to store used newspapers, aluminum, glass and plastic. A recycling bin solves the problem. Unlike the garbage bin, it is divided into sections that neatly separate objects according to the material of which they are made.

## GARBAGE BINS

### FREESTANDING KITCHEN BINS

**Style** Plastic or metal bins for the kitchen.

**In use** There are two main designs; flip-top or pedal. A flip-top (also called a swing bin) is generally 24-28in. high but is available in a smaller size; the hinged lid moves out of the way when garbage is put in. On some models, the lid can be made to stay open.

A pedal bin is usually smaller (around 18in. high). The lid lifts up when the pedal is pressed. Both types of bin can be fitted with bin liners; pedal bins usually have a second inner bin. Both styles of bin are available in a range of colors.

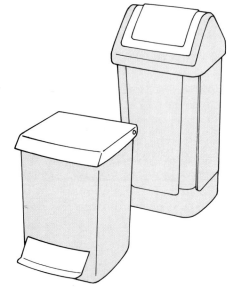

### WALL-MOUNTED BINS

**Style** A plastic bin that can be screwed to the wall. It has a lift-up lid.

**In use** Ideal as a small bin, this type needs one hand to open the bin while the other puts in the garbage. It ranges in size from pedal-bin to flip-top-bin size. Available in a range of colors.

## CONCEALED BINS

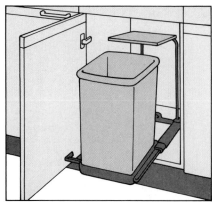

### DOOR BACK STYLE

**Style** Garbage bin fitted to the back of a kitchen unit door.

**In use** When you open the cupboard door the lid on the bin opens too. Usually situated under the sink – this makes good use of a limited amount of space. It also saves floor space.

### PULL-OUT STYLE

**Style** Fitted in a cupboard (mounted on the base of the unit) on its own pull-out sub-frame.

**In use** When the door opens the bin slides out. When you close the door the bin slides back into the cupboard on its frame and goes back into position under the lid (which does not move).

### DRAWER STYLE

**Style** Bin is fitted in a deep drawer unit, which slides out when you pull out the drawer. The lid also pops up when bin is pulled out.

**In use** As with all the concealed bins, the inside of the drawer unit should be cleaned regularly to prevent a musty or moldy smell.

# EXHAUST FANS AND RANGE HOODS

## A guide to the different ways of getting rid of steam, grease and smells.

Cooking smells can permeate the whole house if they are not removed close to the source at the time they are produced. Opening a window or door may help, but in winter this means heat is lost.

If grease-laden air is not removed from kitchens, it will soon deposit itself on wall and ceiling surfaces.

A vent of some sort should be located only 21in. to 30in. away from the cooking surface. This distance may vary depending upon the capacity of the blower, as well as the cook's preference and local code requirements.

Water vapor is one of today's greatest enemies – particularly now that many houses have been well draft-proofed, removing a lot of 'natural' ventilation. If the air inside the house contains too much moisture, this will condense on cold surfaces such as windows or walls, which can lead to serious problems – rotten window frames, peeling wallpaper, black mold and

crumbling plastic. Water vapor is most often created in kitchens and bathrooms – there are a number of steps that can be taken to reduce condensation, but one of the most effective is to remove water vapor at its source.

A simple way of providing a means for air to escape from the kitchen is a **ductless ventilator**. This type of fan is housed in a steel grille that fits directly into the wall. The fan is wired into a junction box and requires no ducting. Many fans are available with a high and a low speed. It is best to place the fan close to the cooking source.

The **trickle ventilator** – is installed in the head of the window or the window-frame. (Many double-glazed windows are supplied with these already built into the frames.) A trickle ventilator is a vent that is open to the elements on the outside of the window but guarded with a cover on the inside – this can be opened and closed by hand as required.

The next step up is an electrically operated ventilator – **an exhaust fan**. This can be fitted in a circular hole cut either in a window or in an outside wall (with a grille on the outside wall). Alternatively it can be fitted in the ceiling, with a duct taking the air to the outside wall or, if upstairs (in the bathroom perhaps), to a vent outlet positioned in a roof tile.

The positioning of an exhaust fan is important. It should be placed on the opposite side of the room to the main source of ventilation – usually an internal door leading into the room – and preferably with the source of water vapor/smells (cooktop, sink, bath) in a line between the two.

Size is also important. A kitchen needs around 10 or more changes of air per hour when it is being used for cooking, so a kitchen measuring 10 × 13ft. with a ceiling 7½ft. high would need a fan capable of moving at least 9660 cubic ft. per hour.

Where an exhaust fan is fitted in a room containing a toilet, which has only a small window (or no window at all), it is wired into the light switch so that it comes on automatically when the room is used and stays on for 15 minutes afterwards. Extracted air is then ducted out through an outside wall. Some exhaust fans can be fitted with humidity sensors so that they come on automatically when the humidity level in the room reaches a certain level – this is useful in bathrooms which tend to be exposed often to dampness.

## TYPES OF VENTILATOR

### DUCTLESS VENTILATOR
**Style** A circular polymeric grille housed in steel. Installed directly in a wall 4 ½-9½in. thick.
**In use** This type of fan requires no ducting and is wired into a junction box. It has only one speed and measures 14in. × 14in. A do-it-yourselfer can handle installation.

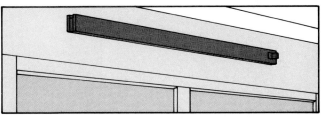

### TRICKLE VENTILATOR
**Style** A two-part ventilator fitted over holes drilled through the head of the window or the window frames. Many aluminum double-glazed window units incorporate ventilators as a standard feature.
**In use** Usually adjustable by a lever, a trickle ventilator can be fitted when you do not want to cut a hole in the window pane. Especially suitable for use in living rooms.
**Watchpoint** Care is needed in drilling holes and any wood exposed should be primed or treated with wood preservative.

## TYPES OF EXTRACTOR FANS

### WINDOW MOUNTED
**Style** Circular, square, or rectangular electrically operated fans fitted into a hole cut in the window.
**In use** An exhaust fan needs to be connected to an electric supply and is operated either by a pull cord on the fan itself or by a separate electric switch on the wall. All are fitted with shutters or louvers

that prevent the wind from blowing in when the fan is not operating.
**Watchpoint** Look for exhaust fans that have multiple speeds.

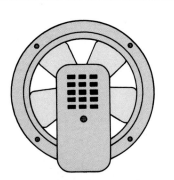

## WALL-MOUNTED

**Style** A rectangular, electrically operated fan mounted directly on an outside wall and connected to a duct.

**In use** The fan is screwed to the inside wall and connected to a short length of ducting that connects in turn to an outlet grille on the outside wall. This is fitted with self-closing louvers. Some wall fans have two or three speeds for greater extraction rates and sometimes a reverse setting that can be used in the summer for cooling the room.

**Watchpoint** Making the large round or rectangular hole necessary for a

wall-mounted fan is a job for a builder.

## CEILING-MOUNTED

**Style** A neat and unobtrusive fan mounted in the ceiling above the source of smells or moisture.

**In use** The particular advantage of a ceiling-mounted exhaust fan is that it can be installed directly over the point where it is needed – useful for a separate shower in a bathroom or bedroom. As well as ordinary exhaust fans, there are ceiling-mounted fans that incorporate a light and are operated from the light switch.

**Watchpoint** Unless exhausting into a well-ventilated loft space, a ceiling-mounted fan will need ducting to be fitted in the space

above the ceiling so that it leads to an outlet grille in the outside wall or roof.

## TYPES OF RANGE HOODS

A range hood is positioned over a range or separate hob to remove water vapor and cooking smells. There are two main types of range hood – ducted and recirculating.

**Ducted range hood** Air is taken through the hood's grease filter (usually made of latex foam, plastic or a similar material) and then it is extracted to the outside air via a lined hole in the wall and an outlet grille. The grease filter should be periodically washed. Generally a hood like this has two or three speeds. It is the more effective type of hood of the two.

**Recirculating range hood** Air is taken through a grease filter then through a charcoal filter, which removes smells and moisture. The 'purified' air is then returned to the room. In other words, the recirculating hood has no duct. As with a ducted range hood it usually has two or three speeds and needs an electrical supply. It has the advantage that it does not need to be fitted against an outside wall.

The performance of this type of range hood is drastically reduced if the filters are not cleaned and/or replaced regularly. Look for charcoal filters which are thick and densely packed for best results.

**Sizes and positioning** Most range hoods are designed to fit under cupboards above the stove, so common sizes are 24in., 36in. and 40in. wide – which match up with kitchen cupboard widths.

The height above the range or hob is important: the normal recommendation is between 24in. and 38in. above the hob, though instructions vary. If the range hood is positioned above a range with an eye-level grill, it should be at least 16in. above the top of the grill (for safety reasons). Most range hoods are installed with lights that can be operated independently of the fan.

**Cooktop downdraft extractor** Where a separate cooktop is positioned in an island unit, or where several hob modules are sited next to one another, an alternative to a range hood is a downdraft extractor sited next to the cooktop itself and connected to a duct that takes the air to the outside via a hole in the wall.

### CONVENTIONAL STYLE

**Style** These are wall-mounted and protrude beyond neighboring cupboards about 6in.

**In use** A pull-out visor extends the depth of the hood – this should be pulled out so that it extracts cooking fumes and steam from the front two hot plates on your cooktop or range.

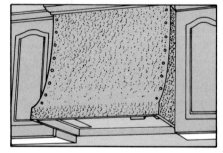

### CANOPY STYLE

**Style** Popularly available in a beaten copper or brass to fit in with 'rustic-style' kitchens.

**In use** All the workings of the hood are hidden under the canopy. The canopy usually extends as high as the top of the adjacent kitchen units. Because of their size, they are very efficient.

### INTEGRATED STYLE

**Style** Installed behind a hinged door or dummy front so they blend in with a built-in kitchen.

**In use** Operated by pulling the base of the door/front outwards so it protrudes over the hob. Usually automatically switches off again when the panel is pushed in.

### TELESCOPIC STYLE

**Style** Built into a wall unit, a slimline flat hood 20in. deep pulls out over the cooktop to trap steam and cooking smells.

**In use** When not in use this can be pushed back in to sit flush with adjacent wall cupboards. Available ducted or recirculating.

### DOWNDRAFT EXTRACTOR

**Style** A slim, slotted powerful extractor fan installed next to the hob surface and sunk below countertop level, leaving only a metal grille exposed.

**In use** This type of extractor is usually fitted as part of the cooktop itself an is connected via ducting to the outside air in much the same way as an exhaust range hood.

**Watchpoint** Although neat and effective, this is very expensive. Because of its position, it does tend to get dirty from cooking spills or grease splashes. However, the grille can be removed and cleaned with a damp cloth.

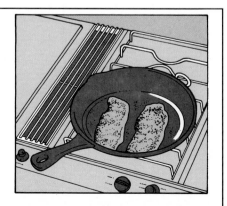

# CHOOSING A DISHWASHER

Dishwashers are a useful piece of kitchen equipment. They can cut down on housework and save hours every week.

A dishwasher can wash, rinse and dry a full load of lightly soiled dishes in just 30 minutes. A hand wash will take up to 90 minutes – saving, on average, up to one hour of your own time each day. This timesaving adds up to more than two weeks over the course of a year.

## SIZE
Most dishwashers are about the same size as a standard washing machine – about 34in. high by 24in. wide by 24in. deep. However, there are compact and portable models available. They usually measure 34in. high by 18in. wide by 25in. deep. This size is perfect for kitchens in which space is a concern. The portable models are available with casters connected and come in both compact and regular sizes. One advantage to having a portable, besides the fact that it can be stored elsewhere, is that it often comes with a laminate or chopping-block top for use as an island.

## CAPACITY
Most standard dishwashers hold 12 international place settings. A setting consists of a dinner plate, soup plate, side plate, cup and saucer, glass, and a set of cutlery. However, one or two manufacturers make slightly larger machines that will take a load of up to 14 place settings.

## CONSTRUCTION
Most machines are front opening with a drop-down door. The inside is normally stainless steel and there are usually two racks – one upper and the other lower – on which to stand the dirty dishes. These sectionalized racks are made of plastic-coated wire and are generally mounted on nylon casters to allow them to slide in and out of the machine for ease of loading. There is a separate container for cutlery, which can sometimes be removed to make room for large pots and pans.

Much of a dishwasher's efficiency depends upon the shape and size of the racks and how easily the jetted water can get at the dirty plates.

## DISHWASHING CYCLE
There are five basic steps in a normal washing program when china, dishes and cutlery are cleaned and dried. These steps are:
☐ Hot water rinse.
☐ Heating – water is heated and controlled by a thermostat.
☐ Washing – all dishwashers use water at high pressure to carry out their cleaning process. The water is distributed in the form of jets passing through rotating spray arms.
☐ Rinsing – the dishes are rinsed with hot water.
☐ Drying – this is carried out either by a fan-assisted heater or by using the residual heat from the hot water after the rinsing cycle.

## FEATURES
Most models have acoustic insulation to keep noise to a minimum during operation, which is important if you don't want to drown your guests' after-dinner conversation. Most models take rinse aid, which prevents spotting on glasses, and have built-in water softeners (usually coarse or granulated salt). These are useful in hard-water areas but the rinse aid and the water softener have to be recharged regularly.

There are a number of finishes to choose from to match the rest of your kitchen: enameled steel, brushed stainless, or even a wood-grain finish.

A variety of features are available depending on the manufacturer. Look for energy-saving features and rack-styles to fit your particular needs.

Also to be found on some machines is an anti-flood facility which makes the machine safer to use at night.

## CYCLES
Most machines offer a variety of cycles to suit different wash loads. However, in practice you really only require a normal, light and intensive wash, plus a rinse-and-hold facility. The latter allows you to build up a full load during the day so that the day's washing can be done all at once. Also useful are the half-load facilities on some makes.

## SITING
Dishwashers can be freestanding or built-in. In the case of the small models they can be put on a table top, draining board or work surface.

## INSTALLATION
Installing a built-in dishwasher is not as difficult as you may think. It requires relatively simple hot-water, drain and electrical connections, as well as a few carpentry techniques.

To start, unpack the machine and carefully go over the manufacturers' installation instructions. The first step you will have to take is to find a place for the washer. Most units fit into a 24in. space, about one cabinet's width.

Keep in mind that you will have to tie in the water and drain lines. Usually the washer is located near the sink, since it is the logical place for it to go, but you may choose to connect the lines to the basement plumbing and in this case you will have to go through the floor.

You also will need a separate 15- or 20-amp branch circuit for electricity.

It is important to check that the water pressure at the point where the machine will be connected is sufficient – check with a plumber before the machine is installed.

## RUNNING COSTS
Many machines have energy-saving features. Electricity accounts for half the running costs, the rest being made up by detergent, water, water softener and rinse aid, so it makes sense to cut down on the cycle times and temperatures of the wash where possible.

## ADVANTAGES
Timesaving is a major advantage and one of the main reasons for investing in a dishwasher. However, it is not the only plus point by any means.

Dishes washed in a dishwasher will literally sparkle when clean. A dish-

## CONSIDERATIONS
It is not recommended to wash the following in your dishwasher:
☐ Dishes with gold, silver or platinum decoration
☐ Lead crystal or delicate glass should not be washed at high temperatures
☐ Bone, ivory or wooden handled utensils
☐ Non-heatproof plastic
**Plus** you should not let stainless steel and silver come into contact with each other in the machine since they trigger off a chemical reaction.

washer will do wonders for every day glasses that will also come out gleaming. If properly loaded, a dishwasher rarely breaks anything and can be used for even your most precious china, provided that it does not have any gold or silver decoration. (See Considerations box on previous page.)

## HYGIENE

A recent survey taken discovered that the bacteria count on handwashed and dried dishes is seven times higher than those washed and dried by machine. This is due to the fact that a machine uses much hotter water.

## SAFETY

Most machines have a cut-out device that will turn off the power if the door is accidentally opened during operation. Some have childproof or retractable controls.

## DISADVANTAGES

You may require extra crockery if you use the machine only once daily.

## MAINTENANCE

Dishwashers require little maintenance, except such things as cleaning the special filters that trap dispersed food particles and refilling the rinse aid. Choosing a well-designed machine with most of its parts accessible from the front will save you time and money.

(See Considerations box on previous page.)

---

### CHECKLIST
Points to look for when choosing your dishwasher:
- ☐ Capacity
- ☐ Kitchen space available
- ☐ Quick wash cycle
- ☐ Quietness
- ☐ Delay timer
- ☐ Childproof locks
- ☐ Anti-flood facility
- ☐ Removable racks/baskets
- ☐ Easy-cleaning facilities
- ☐ Rinse aid
- ☐ Limitations on plate sizes
- ☐ Design of door frame
- ☐ Wash temperatures available

---

## TYPES OF DISHWASHERS

### PORTABLE COMPACT
**Style** This space saving model measures 35in. high by 18in. wide by 25½in. deep. It features a two-level wash and a silverware basket. There are three wash cycles to choose from: heavy-duty, normal and power miser. Porcelain-enameled steel interior resists scratching, peeling and rust. Comes with laminated top and casters for easy transport.
**In use** Perfect for those who live in an apartment or have small kitchens. Since it is portable, it can be disconnected and stored elsewhere.

### FRONT-LOADING MACHINE
**Style** This model is the most commonplace and is approximately the same size as a standard washing machine – usually about 34in. high by 24in. wide by 24in. deep.
   It has a front-opening, drop-down door that when open makes a useful place to put dishes while loading and unloading.

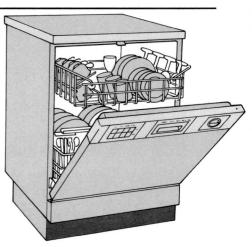

**In use** This type of dishwasher usually takes 12 international place settings, although there are one or two models around which will take 14 settings. Normally there is a range of wash cycles.
**Watchpoint** Some hold plates no bigger than 10in. diameter.

---

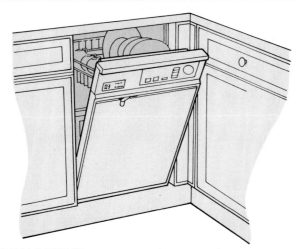

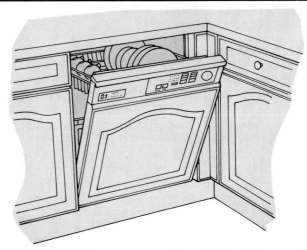

### BUILT-IN COMPACT
**Style** This model is a built-in version of the portable compact described above. It is available with all of the same features, except the laminated top (since it is installed underneath the countertop).
**In use** This is ideal for homes where space is a problem.
**Watchpoints** Since the amount of loading space is limited, this model may not be ideal for larger families.

### INTEGRATED MODELS
**Style** This is a standard size machine that is specially designed to be built into a range of kitchen units. It has a choice of different decor frames into which you can insert your own paneling to match in with the rest of your kitchen units.
**In use** All maintenance and servicing is easily accessible from the front so that the machine does not have to be moved once it is plumbed in.

# UTILITY ROOMS

## A well-designed utility room provides an area for laundry and hobbies, leaving the kitchen free for cooking and eating.

A utility room can house the washing machine and dryer, cleaning equipment, ironing board, and an assortment of tools and materials for the family's various hobbies, together with a place to carry them out. Too often these activities take place in the kitchen, pushing the poor cook into a corner.

It doesn't have to be spacious – even a large cupboard or pantry can be made serviceable – but a utility room does call for careful planning. If you are working with a small area, such as a pantry or a hall cupboard, look for equipment that is stackable.

A self-contained room with space for a washing machine and dryer, a cupboard for cleaning materials and somewhere to keep the ironing board and iron, frees valuable space in the kitchen. An extra sink allows

clothes to be soaked or flowers to be arranged without disrupting the preparation of a meal. The freezer is likely to work more efficiently in a cool utility room than in a hot kitchen.

If you can fit it in, a corner for sewing, with a wide surface to work on, and some shelves or drawers lets you leave work out without cluttering the living room. (Often getting out the machine and setting up takes as much time as the sewing.) If the sewing machine is fixed to a lift-up counter, you can store it neatly when not in use.

**The site** You don't need a small country manor to find space for a utility room.

The back of the garage, one side of a wide corridor, a converted rear hall or entry can all be made serviceable. If there is room, the end of a con-

servatory or sun room, a rarely used dining room or even a downstairs coat closet can be closed off with cupboard doors to conceal a utility area.

A basement or a dry cellar can be turned into a practical and useful hobbies room with all the utility equipment arranged along one wall.

Clever planning allows the utility room to double up for other uses. Kitchen units accommodate large amounts of cleaning equipment and some have special features, such as a fold-out ironing board or a trolley that rolls away neatly under a countertop.

### Well fitted

*The most straightforward way to plumb a room is to run all the pipework along one wall. Here, kitchen units are used to house a stacked washing machine and dryer. The sink has cupboards above and below and the unit at the end is tall enough to hold the ironing board.*

*An adjustable swivel chair and an extra length of work surface opposite creates a sewing center. Add a bulletin board for hanging fabric samples, scissors and patterns.*

## PRACTICAL ASPECTS

Consider the hot and cold water supplies and drainage for the washing machine and sink. Think about where the pipes will have to run and get an estimate for any work from a plumber before you begin. If you are installing a washing machine in a basement you may need to bring waste water up to ground level.

Efficient ventilation is another essential; rust, damp, mildew and condensation are all problems in a badly ventilated utility room. Install an exhaust fan or ventilator grid. Some are linked to the light switch, so they turn on whenever the room is used.

Dryers are usually outfitted with a venting kit to remove the moist, damp air. The tubing either needs to reach across to an open window or can be permanently fitted through an external wall. Some dryers condense the warm air and pump the condensed water out; they need simply to have a waste pipe leading to the main drain.

Allow for plenty of electrical outlets as many of the pieces of equipment will need to remain plugged in all the time. Fit several at counter height too, so you can plug in items such as an iron.

### △ Neatly styled

There was enough room in this rear hall for a short run of kitchen units with a washing machine and tumble dryer behind matching decor panels and a stainless-steel sink with faucet. There is a high shelf for laundry detergent and a steel pole with butchers' hooks for hanging utensils neatly.

### ◁ Simply concealed

Careful choice of well-designed units maximizes storage space. A venetian blind pulls down over the 'hardware' and the ironing board folds back into a cupboard, leaving a room that can be adapted for another use, such as a playroom or hobbies room.

Apricot-colored cupboard doors and a gray-brown tiled floor take the emphasis away from the cold white of the machines.

◁ **Corner cupboard**
There was room in this rarely used dining room to close off an alcove at one end with louvered doors hiding a washing machine, tumble dryer and a shelf for assorted cleaning materials from view.

▽ **Stacked approach**
Alternatively, the dryer can be stacked above the washing machine, freeing the space on the left.

Underneath the counter there is room for a wire trolley with two deep drawers for sorting clothes and piling ironing. Above this is an iron holder and a double outlet. An eye-level, lockable cupboard keeps detergents and cleaning fluids well out of children's reach.

The doors are replaced with solid wood, the left-hand one equipped with two sturdy hooks to hang a collapsible ironing board.

*BRIGHT IDEA*

**Iron holder** Irons, especially steam irons, are best stored upright. A holder mounted on the wall lets you hang up the iron immediately after use. Made of steel, with brackets to wind the cord around, the holder can be hung on a wall or the inside of a cupboard door.

## UTILITY WATCHPOINTS

☐ Washing machines may flood occasionally, so a waterproof floor is essential. Lay ceramic or quarry tiles for long lasting good looks, or cushioned vinyl for warmth and comfort.

☐ Care should be taken to position all switches and outlets well out of the way of any water. Trailing wires should also be avoided.

☐ If machines are built under counters, make sure that they can be pulled out for access to switches and plumbing.

☐ A track of spotlights or a fluorescent strip provides a better level of even light than a single pendant.

### ▷ Picture window
*Brighten up a dark room or one where the window looks out on an uninspiring view with a picture blind.*

*This tiny utility room has a single drainboard sink set into a countertop that continues over a front-loading washing machine and dryer. There is enough room to leave the ironing board standing against the other wall.*

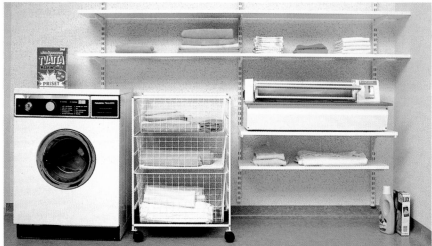

### ◁ Storage solutions
*A place to sort dirty laundry and somewhere to store clothes before ironing is a must. Newly washed laundry should be kept well-aired. Here, plastic-coated wire drawers in a pull-out unit with slatted shelves above ensure nothing is ruined by dampness.*

*Fit narrow shelves and cover with roller blinds if the room is too small for ordinary cupboard doors.*

*If there is room, screw wire racks to the back of the main door, or cupboard doors, to squeeze in extra storage space. Ironing boards, brooms and mops can all be hung from a row of hooks on the wall.*

### ▷ Shower room
*A utility room plumbed for a washing machine could be the ideal place for an extra shower.*

*If you do have a shower in a utility room, you will need to observe the same safety regulations regarding electricity as you do for a bathroom and good ventilation is essential.*

# WASHERS AND DRYERS

The choice is bewildering. Use our guide to help you make the decision on which machine best suits your needs.

## WASHING MACHINES AND DRYERS

The type of washing machine you buy will depend upon the size of your family and the amount of space available in your kitchen or utility room. While most washers do their job equally well, some use more energy and water than others.

A washing machine can be purchased for less than $300 and as much as $800. There are many factors that determine the price.

**Size** Although they are available in a number of odd sizes for installation purposes, most full-sized washers are 27 inches wide. Tubs are usually available in both large and extra large. An extra-large tub uses water, energy and detergent more efficiently than the regular tub, but it does cost extra. The tub, usually made from stainless steel or vitreous enamel, is perforated or slotted.

Manufacturers make other models that are compact, have a built-in dryer on top or can be rolled out and attached to the sink.

**Top-loaders and front-loaders** Top loaders are widely available, while front-loaders are rarely found in this country. Front-loaders can sometimes take a dryer on top, but they are expensive and hold less laundry than top-loaders. Also, front-loaders are more likely to break down.

**Capacity** Most washing machines take an average of 9-18 lbs. of dry laundry while smaller machines will only handle about half of this amount.

**Spin speeds** Water is removed from the clothes by centrifugal force when the tub is rotated at high speed. Thus the faster the spin, the more water is extracted. Two-speed washers generally are more expensive than one-speed washers. The second, slower speed is helpful when washing delicates. It can be applied to different cycles in the wash or to all of the cycles in the wash. The normal speed is fine for most clothing. Some machines are automatic, which means that the speeds are set depending upon the type of wash cycle.

**Energy efficiency** Heating the water for the wash accounts for most of the energy costs, therefore costs depend upon the amount of hot water used. Front-loaders are more frugal when it comes to water use.

**Water extraction** Since wetter laundry takes longer to dry in the dryer, how well a washing machine extracts water affects the amount of energy consumed. Slow spin cycles leave more water.

**Unbalanced loads** Once in a while a heavier load will become unbalanced in the machine. This can cause an excessive amount of noise or, even worse, damage to clothing or the washer itself. It helps to make sure the washer is level. To make leveling easier, some models use a design that attaches the rear legs together, making it easier to level. Be aware that sometimes having the washer on a wood floor amplifies the vibration and noises caused by the machine.

**Special features** There are a few options when it comes to special features.

☐ **Extra temperatures** Usually the three basic wash/rinse choices (hot/cold; warm/cold; and cold/cold) are sufficient, but fancier models feature hot/warm and warm/warm cycles as well.

☐ **Cycles** The three basic cycles are regular, permanent press and delicate. Fancy models have added a soak/pre-wash stage to the cycle or an extra rinse at the end. This can be done on a regular machine by manipulating the dial. Usually temperature and load size are set separately, but on some machines the cycle determines these factors as well.

☐ **Water levels** Most models offer a choice of 3 different levels. This is important since adjusting the fill saves water, energy and detergent. Fancy models offer 4 levels or feature a continuously adjustable control.

☐ **Finishes** Plastic-based finishes have replaced the traditional porcelain finish. They are softer than porcelain but harder than enamel.

☐ **Water temperatures** Some machines are available with an electronic temperature control option. Most machines, however, measure out hot and cold water straight from the house or the water heater. If water is too cold, you may need to use a liquid detergent rather than powder.

☐ **Agitator effects** Circulation must occur in order for a machine to wash effectively. The design of the agitator determines how the laundry will move inside the machine. When the washer is overloaded, the circulation stops and clothing can be damaged. Different manufacturers feature differently designed agitators.

☐ **Electronic controls** Top-of-the-line models feature electronic touchpads rather than the knobs that most machines use to control temperature, water level and spin cycles.

☐ **Extra basket** Some machines come equipped with a small-size basket for mini loads.

**Controls** Machines vary but each is likely to have a single cycle selector dial. Some more sophisticated models have digital push-button control with LED display instead. The most sophisticated even incorporate a special display that indicates that a fault has developed or that an incorrect cycle has been selected – this is all possible thanks to the advent of the microchip!

**Detergents and fabric conditioners** A low-lather detergent should always be used in a front-loading automatic to avoid 'over-sudsing,' which results in a poor wash and can harm the machine.

Detergent dispensers usually have three compartments; one for pre-wash detergent, one for main wash detergent and one for fabric conditioner. Dispensers are filled as required before the machine is switched on and the contents automatically dispensed into the machine at the correct time during the cycle. Some of the full-featured models have a conditioner tank inside the washing machine that only needs to be filled every few months – it adds conditioner automatically each time you

## CHECKLIST

Before buying consider which features you require.

☐ Variety of cycles
☐ High spin speeds
☐ Economy features
☐ Hot and cold water
☐ Childproof features
☐ Automatic timer
☐ Capacity
☐ Separate washer and dryer or a single washer/dryer unit

wash a load of laundry.

**Siting** Front-loading machines can be fitted permanently under a counter whereas top-loading automatics have controls along the back that must be accessible.

Front-loading automatic washing machines and dryers can be 'stacked' one on top of the other. In order to do this, you must buy a 'stacking kit' from the manufacturer. It is best to stack machines that are made by the same manufacturer. However, there is nothing to stop you stacking different makes of machine as long as you check that the sizes are the same and you don't mind that they won't match. An alternative is to buy the combination washer with dryer above.

**Transit bars/brackets** These are supplied by the manufacturer and fitted to the inside of the drum to protect a machine during delivery. They must be removed before use otherwise they can cause damage. Conversely, they must be put back in place if you have to move your machine any distance.

## WASHER-DRYERS

The washer-dryer machine, a popular item in Europe, is rare in this country. This machine, as its name implies, combines the dual functions of washing and drying in one standard-size machine. It is front loading and has a single drum in which both washing and tumble drying take place.

Like the automatic washing machine, the washer-dryer is automatic and works at the touch of a button. A disadvantage to this machine is its inability to dry an entire wash load in one go. Usually some of the clothing must be removed and dried separately.

## TYPES OF AUTOMATIC MACHINES

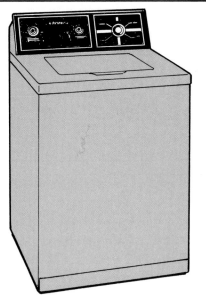

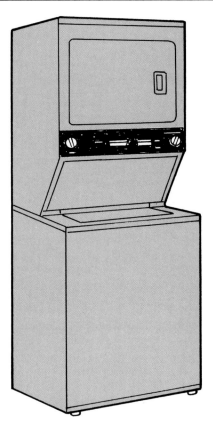

### FRONT-LOADING
Can be freestanding or built in under a work surface. Washing is loaded through the front-opening circular glass door. Controls are situated at the front. Can be stacked with a tumble dryer, using a stacking kit provided by the manufacturer.

### TOP-LOADING
This style opens at the top for easy loading. Special features include a mini-basket tub for small or delicate loads, a filter system for catching lint, a fabric softener dispenser and an extra rinse cycle for added care. Available for electricity or gas.

### PORTABLE COMPACT
This machine can be permanently installed or rolled up to the sink for easy hook-up. A tub fill and drain coupler lets you use the faucet while you are washing. The water temperature is set at the sink. Hoses and power cords are stored at the rear of the washer.

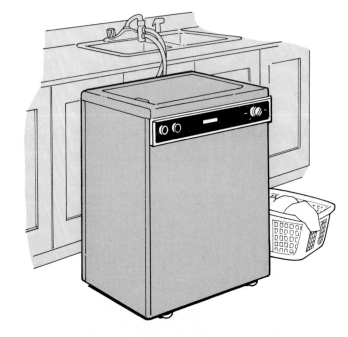

### WASHER-DRYER COMBO
This model features a washer unit on the bottom with a dryer unit above. Thinner than regular styles, this model can be installed in a space just 27in. wide. It is available for electricity or gas.

## DRYERS

When clothes or fabrics have been washed (either by hand or in a washing machine), they are usually still too wet to iron and the quickest and most reliable way to remove this excess water is to use an electric or gas dryer.

Dryers use a combination of heat and mechanical movement to provide quick and even drying. The wet washing is placed in a perforated steel drum through which warm air is passed. Air is drawn into the machine over heating elements and passes through the moving clothes, taking moisture from them. The warm, moist air must then be removed from the machine.

With today's variety of fabrics, temperature control is the key to drying clothing. For example, cottons can withstand high temperatures, but permanent press items must be warmed to relax wrinkles and then cooled down before new wrinkles set into the fabric. Delicates, such as lingerie, require very little heat and rubber and plastic items should be run in the 'fluff' or 'air dry' cycle.

## VENTING DRYERS

The dryer is vented to the outside through an exhaust outlet. Unless the room is particularly large and well ventilated, a venting kit will be necessary — basically, this is a pipe or tube, which is usually sold separately from the machine. The pipe is usually flexible, but can be fixed.

**Flexible** A large, flexible tube about 4in. in diameter is attached to the front, back, or side of the dryer and the free end may be hung through a door or window. The tubing can be removed and stored when not in use.

**Fixed** A large diameter tube attached to the machine can be built through an outside wall as a permanent vent.

**Safety** It isn't advisable to put a dryer in a bathroom for safety reasons. However it is possible to get around this problem by connecting it to a fixed switched spur outside the room and enclosing it in a cupboard.

**Sizes** Dryers are available in different sizes ranging from fairly small models which can be wall-mounted to others designed to fit beneath a standard 36in-high countertop. To save space many models may be stacked on top of a washing machine.

**Capacity** The amount of washing which can be dried at a time varies from model to model but ranges between 6lbs. and 18lbs. For best results it is important not to overload the machine. It is usually better to dry two smallish loads rather than one large one, especially in the case of man-made fibers which are particularly prone to creasing.

**Operation** A dryer's control panel is simple and to the point. It consists of a rotary dial for automatic and timed cycles and other knobs and buttons to set temperature. Throughout a cycle the dial provides a rough idea of where the laundry is within the cycle. This can be helpful if drying unusual or extremely delicate clothing that requires supervision. Unlike a touchpad or a more elaborate control panel, these simple dials and knobs are relatively easy to service.

**Moisture-sensors** New technology has made possible a dryer that uses sensors to measure moisture directly. Sensors inside the drum actually touch the clothing and determine its moisture content. Moisture-sensing models are more efficient as they shut off as soon as they sense the clothing is dry.

**Crease prevention** Some machines have an anti-crease cycle which uses a cool, intermittent 'reverse tumble action' at the end of the timed cycle to prevent excessive creasing.

**Advantages** Dryers can remove several pints of water in a relatively short space of time, but they only work really efficiently if the clothes have already been well spun. If, for example, you put clothes into the dryer which haven't first been spun, not only will they take a *very* long time to dry properly, but the electricity used is going to be far more — and certainly not cost-effective.

## TYPES OF DRYERS

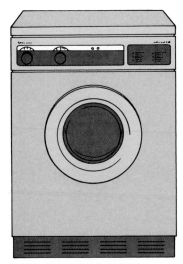

**VENTED – FIXED OR FLEXIBLE**
**Style** The moist air removed from the clothes is discharged through an air outlet which, unless the room is particularly large and well ventilated, needs to be removed through an outside wall. This can be done by a permanent pipe/hose or via a flexible one which is just pushed through an open window.
**In use** A 'venting kit' from the manufacturer is not usually supplied with the machine so is an extra cost. Fixed venting requires making an additional permanent escape route to the outside. A dryer could be used in a closet.

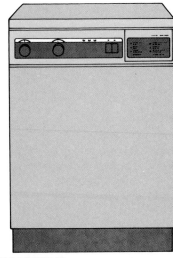

**TOP-LOADING**
**Style** This type is freestanding and must be installed in a space where nothing will hang above it. Usually partnered with matching washing machine.
**In use** Moisture-sensing models, those that actually sense the amount of moisture left in the clothing, are available. This prevents overdrying.
Models also feature variable temperature control and timed cycles.

## CHECKLIST

Before making your final choice of dryer consider the availability of the following and their importance to you:
☐ Capacity
☐ Sensor control
☐ Delay timer
☐ Reverse tumble action
☐ Range of drying times
☐ Color of appliance
☐ Will it stack on top of your washing machine?

If you want the two machines to stack neatly, you should probably buy a dryer which is the same make as your washer.

# INDEX

## PHOTOGRAPHIC CREDITS

American Olean Tile Co., 42, 47, 63 (bottom)
American Standard, 39 (top left and right)
B & Q DIY Supercentres, 33
Be Modern, 66 (top left)
Bosch, 24 (bottom), 39 (bottom), 66 (top right)
Bulthaup, 44-45, 88 (top)
Cover Plus from Woolworth, 29 (bottom)
CP Hart/Aqua Ware, 37 (bottom), 50 (bottom)
Cristal Tiles, 54 (top)
Dulux, 89
Elfa Systems, 90 (middle)
Phillip H. Ennis Photography, 24 (top), 31, 43, 63 (top)
EWA, 62, 66 (bottom)
EWA/Michael Dunne, 18 (right), 48-49, 52 (top), 64 (bottom)
EWA/Clive Helm, 51, 57 (top)
EWA/Rodney Hyett, 6, 23, 40 (bottom right), 46, 88 (bottom)
EWA/Neil Lorimer, 52 (bottom)
EWA/Michael Nicholson, 36, 43 (top)
EWA/Spike Powell, 30 (bottom), 53, 90 (top)
EWA/Jerry Tubby, 65 (top)
Formica Ltd., 54 (bottom)
General Electric, 38
Habitat, 34
Hygena, 4-5
Jalag/Zuhause, 14, 15, 18 (top right), 56 (top)
Kohler Co., 17 (top), 28, 39 (top center), 61 (bottom)
Kraftmaid, 40
Leicht Kitchens, 2-3
Miele, 37, 87
Melabee Miller, 64 (top)
Moben Kitchens, 58 (top left)
National Kitchen & Bath Association, 54 (top)
National Magazine Co/David Brittain, 19
National Magazine Co/Jan Baldwin, 59, 60-61
National Magazine Co/Good Housekeeping, 41
NuTone, 30
The Original Kitchen, 50 (top)
Richard Paul, 61 (bottom)
Poggenpohl, 26-7, 29 (top), 45 (top right)
PWA International, 55, 90 (bottom)
PWA/Living magazine, 21
Schreiber Furniture Ltd, 13
SieMatic, 39 (bottom left), 57 (bottom)
Smallbone of Devizes, front cover photograph, 22, 32
Jerry Tubby/Eaglemoss, 35
Ulrich Inc., 17 (bottom), 20, 25, 58 (bottom)
Vymura International, 40 (top)
Winchmore, 16
Woodstock, 1, 34 (bottom), 56 (bottom), 58 (top right)
Wrighton International, 18 (bottom)

## DESIGNER CREDITS:

Mary Jean Kamin, 28
Susan Kelly, 24 (top)
Sharon M. Pretto, 31
NDM Kitchens, Inc., 43 (bottom)
Stephen and Gail Huberman Designs, 63 (top)
The Original Dome Ceiling, Inc., 47
Robert Valleau, 64 (top)
Robert L. Wieland, 54 (top)
Michael Wiener, 17 (top)